THε
GεNεSIS
of SεX

THE
GENESIS
of SEX

SEXUAL RELATIONSHIPS IN
THE FIRST BOOK OF THE BIBLE

O. PALMER ROBERTSON

P&R
PUBLISHING
P.O. BOX 817 • PHILLIPSBURG • NEW JERSEY 08865-0817

Page design by Tobias Design
Typesetting by Michelle Feaster

Printed in the United States of America

Library of Congress Cataloging-in-Publication Data

Robertson, O. Palmer.
    The Genesis of sex : sexual relationships in the first book of the Bible / O. Palmer Robertson.
        p. cm.
    Includes bibliographical references (p.) and index.
    ISBN 0-87552-519-9 (pbk.)
    1. Bible. O.T. Genesis—Criticism, interpretation, etc. 2. Sex in the Bible. 3. Sex—Biblical teaching. I. Title.

BS1235.2.R63 2002
222'.11083067—dc21

                                        2001055459

CONTENTS

CONTENTS

INTRODUCTION

When God first created man, he assigned him three great areas of responsibility. First, man was given the privilege and the responsibility of *worshipping his Creator*. Under this *worship mandate*, man had the responsibility of adoring God as the source of all the blessings he received in life. By blessing the sabbath day and making it holy, the Lord God set apart this day for man to honor his Creator (Gen. 2:3). Secondly, man was given the *marriage mandate*. According to this ordering, the Creator commissioned mankind to "be fruitful and multiply, and fill the earth" (Gen. 1:28 RSV). Implied in this mandate was the Creator's will for man in the whole of the sexual relationship. Thirdly, God gave man the *cultural mandate*. As the crown of all earthly creatures, man was entrusted with the responsibility of subduing the earth to the glory of God (Gen. 1:28c). All the potentialities of the whole of creation were made available to man, to be employed to the fullest to the glory of God.

The second of these creational ordinances is the focus of the present work. Sadly, the world today has virtually lost all touch with the concerns of the Almighty Creator in the realm of human sexuality. The whole world of relations between the sexes is viewed as a purely secularistic thing. If a fool is properly defined as a person who says in his heart, "There is no God" (Ps. 14:1), then in the realm of human sexuality modern man may rightly be viewed as a "ship of fools" tossed about on the sea of life's disordered passions.

In the confused state of today, some people would want to deny the very existence of sex. Others would make a god of sex.

Between these extremes lies a sane view of sex that recognizes the many ways in which sex as a part of God's good creation exercises a significant role in human life.

Appropriately, one of the fullest treatments of the subject of sex is found in the biblical book of Genesis. For this opening piece of literature in the Bible presents itself as the "book of beginnings." The phrase "these are the generations of" occurs ten times in the book of Genesis, marking ten "generatings" that provide insight into origins that can help explain the current state of the world.[1] In this context of human beginnings, virtually every kind of sexual relationship that may be imagined finds its place in the narrations of Genesis. The book opens with a presentation of the creational ordering of marriage and then moves in a most natural way through instances of romance, the love-triangle, singleness, divorce, unrequited love, adultery, rape, and numerous other manifestations of human sexuality. Often these treatments appear in rather full detail.

Many insights helpful for modern man in his confusion over sex will become apparent to the student of this "narrative theology" in Genesis, where the truth of God becomes inescapably transparent in narrative form. In addition, wisdom will be gained for the generations to come about this most important of subjects, a subject in which God the Creator, Christ the Redeemer, and the sanctifying Holy Spirit have a vital concern.

The present study will examine over twenty varieties of sexual relationships as they appear in the book of Genesis. Attention will be focused not narrowly on the idea of sex as "physical contact between individuals involving sexual stimulation," but more broadly on the concept of sex as "manifestations or consequences of sexual instincts, desires, etc."[2] In the process, it is hoped that Genesis as the biblical book of beginnings will supply the kind of healthy understanding of sex so desperately needed in the modern world.

ONE

SEX AND THE BEGINNINGS OF LIFE

■ ■ ■ ■ ■

THE DESIGN OF THE CREATOR

THE DESIGN OF THE CREATOR

I shall make a helper corresponding to the man.
—Genesis 2:18*

The Creator himself declared that it was not good for the man to be alone (Gen. 2:18). Yet no creature on earth could be found that was suitable as a partner for him (Gen. 2:20b). Dogs, cats, parrots, horses, snakes, fish—all these creatures of the animal world have become pets of mankind. But a pampered pet is not an equal partner. So in the beginning God made a "helper corresponding to the man." This new creation was perfectly suited to the man, for the woman was taken from the man, assuring the uniqueness, the intimacy, and the permanence of their relationship (Gen. 2:21–23).

The detailed narrative describing the creation of woman underscores her significance in God's purposes in creation. As one commentator notes: "Genesis 2 is unique [in] . . . the whole of the Ancient Near East in its appreciation of the meaning of woman."[1] The approval by God of this first sexual relationship is vivified by the statement that the Lord himself brought the woman to the man (Gen. 2:22). As Jewish tradition has expressed it, "God acts . . . as *best man* for the first human couple."[2] The depth of the marriage relationship is seen in the fact that a man is commanded to leave the bond between himself and his parents, but never to leave

---

* Scripture quotations marked by an asterisk are the author's translation.

the bond established between himself and his wife. The union established in marriage is deeper than any other human relationship, exceeding the attachment of children to parents, and even parents to children.[3] This intensive bonding finds its origin in the process by which the woman was formed out of the man. Though perhaps stretching a bit the significance of Eve's origin from the rib of Adam, the remark of Matthew Henry is worth noting for its quaintness if for nothing else:

> Not made out of his head to top him, not out of his feet to be trampled upon by him, but out of his side to be equal with him, under his arm to be protected, and near his heart to be beloved.[4]

As another commentator has noted:

> Whence comes this love "strong as death" (S. of Sol. 8:6) and stronger than the tie to one's own parents, whence this inner clinging to each other, this drive toward each other which does not rest until it again becomes one flesh in the child? It comes from the fact that God took woman from man, and they actually were originally *one* flesh.[5]

Because man was designed as a social creature, God made a counterpart for him. And what a mate he made! The wonder of this person who was made for the man has been immortalized in John Milton's description of Adam's first impression of Eve when he awoke from his deep sleep:

Man-like, but different sex, so lovely fair
That what seemed fair in all the world seemed now
Mean, or in her summed up, in her contained
And in her looks, which from that time infused
Sweetness into my heart, unfelt before,
And into all things from her air inspired
The spirit of love and amorous delight.

. . . .

Grace was in all her steps, heav'n in her eye,
In every gesture dignity and love.[6]

The internal structuring of the marriage relationship as intended by the Creator is fully summarized in the description of the woman in relation to the man. She is made as a "helper corresponding to" the man. The perfect balance of a proper relationship between husband and wife may be seen in the fact that the woman is to be a "helper" to the man, while also "corresponding to" him. She is to be his "helper," but equal to him in personhood. This ordering finds confirmation in the new covenant when the apostle Paul states that the man was not created for the woman, but the woman for the man (1 Cor. 11:9). At the same time, though the woman is not independent of the man, so also the man is not independent of the woman (1 Cor. 11:11). The woman was designed by the Creator specifically to be a help to the man in bringing the creation to its consummation goal. She stands as the man's equal in her personhood, having been made in the image of the Creator just as much as was the man. Only as the woman realizes her full potential as a person created in God's image can she properly fulfil her intended role as helper to the man.

The original charge given to the man and the woman was that they "be fruitful, and multiply, and replenish the earth, and subdue it" (Gen. 1:28 KJV). As John Calvin has noted, God himself could have covered the earth with a multitude of human beings without a great deal of trouble. But instead he willed that all mankind "proceed from one fountain, in order that our desire for mutual concord might be the greater, and that each might the more freely embrace the other as his own flesh."[7] Since all people have a common ancestry by the Creator's design, they should have an innate sense of caring for one another. This care for one another embraces the original mandate given mankind to "subdue the earth," so that inequalities which would deny any person sufficient space on the earth to survive are "nothing else than a corruption of nature which proceeds from sin."[8]

These original principles of creation concerning God's institution of marriage receive elaboration and development in the context of the new covenant. Despite man's fall into sin, the expected circumstance is that people be married. But the apostle Paul explains that because of the "present crisis," and by reason of a special "gift," it is good for some people not to marry (1 Cor. 7:1, 7, 26).

So the original ordering of the Creator presumes that one man shall be united to one woman with the result that the two shall become one flesh (Gen. 2:24; cf. Mark. 10:7–8). From the beginning it was God's intent that two and only two become one flesh, as is clearly demonstrated in the fact that God made only one woman to be partner to the one man. Together these two are given the charge by God to multiply, to replenish the earth, and subdue it (Gen. 1:28). Yet in view of the fact that God originally created the man as a complete entity in himself, the single state also can be blessed of Him.

TWO

SEX AND MARRIAGE

■ ■ ■ ■ ■

THE PREARRANGED MARRIAGE
ROMANCE AND MARRIAGE
THE CONSEQUENCES OF MARRIAGE CHOICES
THE LOVE-TRIANGLE
THE MARRIAGE OF BELIEVER TO UNBELIEVER
THE MISMATCHED MARRIAGE
UNREQUITED LOVE
THE FAMILY CONNECTION
DIVORCE
THE SECOND MARRIAGE

THE PREARRANGED MARRIAGE

The LORD God . . . brought her to the man.
—Genesis 2:22

In the free world of today, the selection of a marriage partner is regarded as one of the premier decisions of life. Although the choice may be limited by social status, wealth, local custom, family pressures, and a host of other factors, the right of personal decision in the realm of marital commitment is generally held as sacrosanct.

But through long ages past, and probably in the case of the majority of marriages around the world even into the present day, personal preference regarding a marriage partner has not been the decisive factor. Instead, the marriage of two people has been arranged for them by members of the family or by counselors and friends.

In the Western mind, molded by the Enlightenment, the idea of a prearranged marriage is simply unthinkable. How could a person trust the decision of others in an area that has immeasurable consequences for the whole of the future? Is it even conceivable that two people could be committed to each other for life without having had the opportunity to become acquainted with one another through a process of courtship that eventually led to mutual consent? In one classic case that ended in disaster, an English family of nobility arranged the marriage of their son to the daughter of a monied family from America. The daughter refused to consent to the arrangement until her mother locked her in a room and denied her food and water. But after bearing an heir, the girl divorced her husband and proceeded to marry the man of her choice from France.

The thinking of many people in the world of today may reject outright the concept of the prearranged marriage. But from the beginning it has not been so. As a matter of fact, the book of Genesis records a number of marriages that were arranged apart from the prior decision of bride and groom. Since this type of marriage union will be the experience of many people even in today's world, it may be useful to review the circumstances surrounding a few of the prearranged marriages recorded in the Scriptures.

Is it not a matter of some significance that the first of human marriages was prearranged? God decided that it was not good for Adam to be alone (Gen. 2:18a). God determined to make a helper corresponding to the man (Gen. 2:18b). God formed Eve in a very specific way that she might be the perfect companion to Adam (Gen. 2:21–22a). God brought Eve to Adam, and presented her to him (Gen. 2:22b). God never asked Adam whether Eve should be tall or short in stature, dark or light in complexion. The whole of the process was ordered by the Lord. Neither Adam nor Eve had a single decision to make in the matter. The whole of the union was prearranged on their behalf.

The marriage of Isaac and Rebekah stands out in the book of Genesis as a marriage arranged completely by people other than the bride and the groom. At the same time, the role of God's providence in arranging this marriage deserves special notice. Unbelief leads many to disregard the involvement of God in the ordering of a specific marriage relationship. But the testimony of this particular incident underscores just how far the concern of the Lord goes in this most human of personal relationships. As John Calvin says:

> Irreligious men, partly because they do not hold marriage sufficiently in honour . . . wonder that . . . the Spirit of God should be employed in affairs so minute; but if we have that reverence which is due in reading the Sacred Scriptures, we shall easily understand that here is nothing superfluous: for inasmuch as men can scarcely persuade themselves that the Providence of God extends to marriages, so much the more does Moses [as author of this narrative] insist on this point.[1]

God's hand of providence in the marriage of Isaac and Rebekah is fully evident. Abraham's servant must journey to the homeland of the patriarch's relatives and return with a bride for Isaac (Gen. 24:3–4). After identifying Rebekah as the proper prospective bride, the servant addresses his proposal not to the bride-to-be but to her family. It is Rebekah's brother and father, Laban and Bethuel, that make the critical determination, and in no uncertain terms:

> Here is Rebekah; take her and go, and let her become the wife of your master's son, as the LORD has directed. (Gen. 24:51)

It is true that Rebekah is given some option in the matter (Gen. 24:55–58). But it is her relatives, not the prospective bride herself, who make the initial commitment for her to travel to unknown parts and marry a man she has never seen.

And what about the groom? It would seem that Isaac had less rather than more input into the upcoming marriage. When the servant returned with a new bride in tow, the groom had no decision to make. So "she became his wife, and he loved her" (Gen. 24:67). It was just as simple as that. The whole affair was totally arranged. Isaac and Rebekah had never seen one another, and yet they were committed in marriage.

Now what was the outcome of this prearranged marriage in which neither bride nor groom had ever even seen one another before they were committed irreversibly? So far as the narrative of Genesis reports, this marriage was one of the smoothest, most cordial of relationships found in Scripture. Not only did Isaac love Rebekah devotedly; he found comfort from her in the great sorrows that had overwhelmed him at the death of his mother Sarah (Gen. 24:67c). In addition, nothing is ever said about Isaac's taking another wife alongside Rebekah. In contrast with his father Abraham, who had several wives and concubines, and in contrast with both his sons Jacob and Esau, who had multiple marriages, Isaac apparently found complete contentment in his one bride, the wife of his (relative) youth (cf. Gen. 25:6; 29:28; 30:3, 9; 26:34; 28:8–9; 36:2–3). All during the years of Rebekah's barrenness, it is never reported that Isaac fell into the trap of seeking to solve his problem through the multiplying of wives to himself.

The whole of the circumstance surrounding the marriage of Isaac and Rebekah speaks well of the prearranged marriage. God has his way of ordering things even when they seem to be out of the control of his chosen people. Abraham's servant gave full recognition to the Lord's involvement by his prayer to God and his confession to Rebekah's family (Gen. 24:12–14, 45). His testimony evoked a similar witness from Rebekah's brother and father: "This is from the LORD; we can say nothing to you one way or the other" (Gen. 24:50). God's hand is not limited to working only through the self-conscious decisions of the people most directly affected even by events as significant as marriage.

In an entirely different set of circumstances, Isaac's son Jacob also finds himself committed in a prearranged marriage. In this case, the situation is not quite so happy. Rebekah has sent her son away so that he might find a wife from among her relatives rather than from among the nearby Canaanites (Gen. 27:46–28:3). Jacob promptly falls in love with the beautiful Rachel and happily serves for seven years to gain his heart's desire. The whole long period seemed to Jacob as though it were only a few days because of his love for Rachel. But on the morning after the nuptial vows have finally been taken and the marriage consummated, Jacob discovers to his dismay that he has been wed to Rachel's older sister Leah (Gen. 29:23–25).

Similar circumstances may arise even in the "enlightened" twenty-first century. Parents may arrange a marriage to someone in a nearby town or village. But suppose that one of the parties of the proposed marriage has a deep conviction that living with the other person will prove unendurable. What should be done? In most cultures, the parties of an arranged marriage are allowed to express their opinions. The hope is that a disagreeable arrangement can be avoided.

But suppose the parents are non-Christian, and pursue an arrangement for their Christian son or daughter to be married to a non-Christian. In such cases it may be necessary for the Christian to refuse the proposed arrangement, despite the complications that could arise.

What should Jacob have done in response to his father-in-law's trickery of substituting Leah for Rachel? Scripture reports what he actually did. He contracted with Laban to serve another seven years for the privilege of marrying Rachel, the woman whom he loved.

But what should he have done? Possibly he could have sought an annulment of his marriage to an unwanted bride that had been joined to him through the worst kind of deceit. But most likely the custom of the day would have forbidden this way out of an undesirable situation. In addition, the consummation of the marriage relationship would have made the rightness of this procedure at least questionable.

Given a circumstance in which there was no way out, Jacob should have accepted this arrangement as an appointment of the Lord, and moved on with his life in faith. He had been the deceiver in the past, but he had been outdone, and had reaped what he had sowed. The creational ordinance that a man is to cleave to his wife anticipates the exhortation of the apostle Paul that husbands are to love their wives even as Christ loved the church and gave himself up for her (Gen. 2:24; Eph. 5:25). No doubt the sinners that Christ has bought with his own blood do not always seem lovely to him. Yet he continues to love them nonetheless. The obligation, the privileged commission of husbands, applies not only to marital situations in which all the attendant circumstances suit the taste of a man. The responsibility of a husband to live in love toward his wife goes to the point of requiring that the man be ready to sacrifice his own personal tastes for the one to whom he is wed.

Leah's instinct that she ought to have been loved by her husband Jacob despite the irregularity of their union was a right one. For even the Lord himself intervened in the situation in which she was unloved, and opened her womb while keeping Rachel's closed for many years (Gen. 29:31, 33). "Surely my husband will love me now" was the cry of a woman who had been slighted by the one person in her life who should have loved her more than anyone else (Gen. 29:32).

It might be assumed that people would be quite satisfied if they only knew that God himself had arranged their marriage. But people generally are not content to entrust themselves to the Lord's determinations. For man consistently ranks his will higher than the will of God. One of the earliest indicators of human depravity may be seen in the decision of men before the flood to marry any of the beautiful women they chose, without any concern about God's desire in the matter (Gen. 6:2). Despite the fact that God's will in marriage always is best, people insist on breaking away from any and all restrictions to do what their will concludes shall please them most.

A proper reading of the providential workings of God should encourage a large measure of trust in the Lord's good purposes in the prearrangement of marriages. Few things will encourage people to live contentedly in the circumstance in which they find themselves more than a confident assurance that God has planned their marriage—or their singleness, as the case may be. By trusting in the Lord and committing all our ways to him, we may move ahead in life with the confidence that he is the one that ultimately will determine our marital state. For without putting the blame on God for any sinful human relationships, all marriages ultimately may be viewed as predetermined by the Lord.

A man who had served as an elder in the church for a number of years informed his young pastor that he was divorcing his wife. The minister asked the reason.

"I don't love her anymore," was the response.

"Then love her!" retorted the minister.

The man looked puzzled. "But I don't love her," he replied.

"Then LOVE HER! Scripture says, 'Husbands, love your wives.' So love her."

The point of the young minister was well taken. Love is not merely a matter of emotions, of fickle feelings that come and go. Love is also a matter of the will, the intellect, and the doing of deeds of love. You may ponder long and hard over the question of whether it is God's will that you should marry a certain person. But once you are married, clearly it is God's will that you be married to that particular individual. In this light, your obligation is clear. As a husband, you are to love the person who is your wife, and no other. You are not to return to the fifteenth anniversary celebration of your high school graduating class and think, "Perhaps I should have married that person, or that other one over there." No, you are to be married to the person to whom you are married, and to no other.

So, love your wife. Bring her flowers, perfume, and sweets (if she likes them). If she would prefer something like a Swiss army knife or a new panga blade, get one for her. Cook a meal for her, and wash the dishes afterwards. Bathe the children and do some chores around the house. Be affectionate. Remember her birthday and don't forget the date of your anniversary. Tell her and retell her that you love her, in as many ways as possible.

In the same way, the wife has the obligation to persevere in the relationship with her husband. She is to cultivate a respect and a love for her spouse, without looking for an easy way out of a difficult situation.

Whether the situation seems good or bad, faith will accept the circumstances of a prearranged marriage as coming from the hand of the Lord. In one sense it may be said that all marriages are "prearranged" by him who "works out everything in conformity with the purpose of his will" (Eph. 1:11). A commitment to follow in the ways ordered by the Lord will make a person "more than conqueror" through the one who loves his people with an undying love.

■ ■ ■ ■ ■

ROMANCE AND MARRIAGE

So Jacob served seven years to get Rachel, but they seemed like
only a few days to him because of his love for her.
—Genesis 29:20

Many people tend to go dreamy-eyed the moment the subject of romance is mentioned. So right away a few hard facts about romance need to be noted:

1. You can fall in love with the *right* person before marriage.
2. You can fall in love with the *wrong* person before marriage.
3. You can fall in love with the right person *after* you are married (that is, with your spouse).
4. You can fall in love with the *wrong* person after you are married (that is, with anyone other than your spouse).

With these facts in mind, consider the subject of sex and romance as it appears first in the book of Genesis. Some poor "benighted souls" (a graphic old English way of saying "people who live so much in the dark that they don't have a clue") would deny the reality of romance. But the Bible quite regularly speaks in a variety of ways about people's "falling in love." Of course, the state of being in love is not always presented as inherently good. David's son Amnon "fell in love" with his half-sister Tamar. He was so much in love that he became sick over the girl. But after forcing himself on her, he hated her with a greater passion than he had previously loved her (2 Sam. 13:1–15).

Yet the reality and validity of romantic love are regularly recognized in the Bible. A clear example may be seen in the marriage of Isaac and Rebekah (Gen. 24). The encounter of these two people with one another displays many elements that make for romance.

First, Isaac appears as a man seeking a woman suitable for himself. Sometimes the right one appears without a person's even searching. But the much more normal situation is for a person to be looking for a partner. It is something of a natural thing for single people to ask (secretly to themselves) as they meet new people of the opposite sex, "Could this be the one person meant for me?" A thousand nos to that question will not keep a person from checking out the third finger on the left hand and then asking still again, "Is this the one?"

In Isaac's case, the seeking was done by proxy. Abraham commissioned his servant to go back to his homeland on a mission of finding a wife for his son Isaac. Because he was the only son of Abraham and Sarah, the partner had to be exactly right.

The unnamed servant took his task most seriously, and traveled to the distant country with great trepidation. But his prayers for God's guidance were answered in wondrous ways. The old King James Version of the Bible captures something of the dynamics of the interplay between human initiative and divine direction. In explaining to Abraham's uncle how he ended up at this distant doorstep, the servant says, "I being in the way, the Lord led me" (Gen. 24:27). In this case, the translation happens to be a quite literal rendering of the original Hebrew text.

The phrase has captured a balanced perspective on romantic love when it is rightly ordered of God. The servant, representing the wishes of Isaac his master, is "in the way." He is traveling, looking, searching, checking out prospects. In most cases, that is the way it happens. At least one or the other of a couple is looking, checking out the possibilities, being open to any and all options. Most recently the place to look seems to be the Internet. Numbers of individuals have discovered their perfect partner by means of a little electronic browsing. In any case, if someone is not looking, then a "finding" is not quite so likely to occur.

At the same time, the Lord must lead. As the servant was in

the way, the Lord led him. Earnest, repeated, persistent prayer must be offered that the Lord will lead a person by the orderings of providence to just that person who is meant for him or her. Don't expect a divine, revelatory word that whispers, "This is the one, and the name is 'Chris' (or 'José' or 'Chimwemwe')." But providential directions can provide all the essential factors. The Lord has his own way of arranging the things that bring two people, possibly from widely diverse locales and circumstances, to a single time and place. God has been doing it over the centuries, and he is quite capable of doing it one more time. Trust him! He can manage it. Don't let people put you in a panic. But at the same time, be on the lookout.

Secondly, the woman in particular (but the man as well) must be quite adventurous, willing to take a life-determining risk by committing herself to a relationship on the most intimate level with a person she can at best know only partially. Accept the fact. You are not going to know everything about the other person until *after* marriage. Commitment to wedlock is indeed one of the largest acts of faith a person will ever undertake.

Rebekah's case is quite remarkable and displays her strong faith in God's good will for her life. She had displayed her youthful vivacity at the first meeting with Abraham's servant when she provided him with drink and then proceeded to water all his camels. When the decision regarding a delay of the journey is put to Rebekah, she does not hesitate. She agrees to travel the very next morning with a servant she has just met to a land she has never seen in order to marry a man about whom she knows very little. Although the marriage relationship normally is based on quite a bit more firsthand knowledge of the proposed spouse than in the case of Isaac and Rebekah, still there is always the element of risk. Unending delay will not solve the problem. Even going so far as engaging in premarital sexual relations in an effort to ascertain adequate compatibility cannot guarantee a good match. In some cultures it is the custom for a woman to get pregnant before a marriage in order to prove that she can have children. But these unbiblical tactics only undermine the psychological basis for the lifetime commitment that is necessary for making a marriage work. Nothing can substitute for strong faith in the good purposes of the Lord. In any case, the Christian believer must not submit to unbiblical customs, whatever the cost.

Thirdly, romantic love does not automatically exclude parental involvement in the commitment of marriage. Rebekah's parents approve the relationship before she cuts her ties and travels to unknown parts to marry an unknown man. In a similar way, the narrative ends by noting that Isaac took Rebekah "into the tent of his mother" (Gen. 24:67). This action indicates that he sought and received parental approval before the marriage was consummated. The very healthy but nonetheless earthy depiction of marriage found in the Song of Songs indicates the same thing. This time it is the bride who leads her husband to the house of her mother, the one who had taught her (Song 8:2).

A healthy dose of romance in marriage does not require sneaking behind the backs of family members and trusted friends. As a matter of fact, romance in marriage most often will come into fullest bloom in an environment in which relationships among family and friends are properly maintained. Given an approving context in which negative social static is absent, romantic love will be experienced in its most satisfying form.

Fourthly, romantic love always will contain that mysterious, indefinable element that makes it all the more pleasurable and exciting. The most rational, logical of human beings may be the very person most strongly struck by the romance of love. Look at this fellow! He's always got his nose in a book. He never looks up when a pretty girl passes by. She may be wearing her high-heel shoes that click along the library floor. She wears a flattering dress and a nice perfume. Still he keeps on thumbing through his stack of books. But then one day, *BANG!* It's all over for him. As the old saying goes, "The bigger they are, the harder they fall."

Just at the time that Rebekah was completing her long journey, Isaac had gone out into the field to "meditate" (Gen. 24:63). This particular word occurs only in this passage in the Old Testament. The context would seem to be hinting rather strongly about the subject of his meditation. As one commentator has noted, "Isaac probably was restless as he awaited the return of his father's servant, so he spent some time by himself quietly contemplating what the future might hold for him."[2] Another commentator is more explicit, noting that Isaac had gone into the field at evening time "undoubtedly to lay the question of his marriage before God in solitude."[3] As he looked up and saw his father's trusted servant coming, he might have seen at a distance his prospective bride spring lightly from her camel. At the same time, Rebekah asked if the lone figure standing in the field was her husband-to-be. Learning of his identity, she quickly placed a veil over her face since something of the air of mystery about marriage had to remain until after the sealing service had been completed.

The narrative of Isaac and Rebekah concludes by noting that "she became his wife, and he loved her" (Gen. 24:67). This little phrase says it all. Isaac loved Rebekah. He was totally taken up with her. In other words, he "fell in love" with her—*after marriage!* He couldn't get enough of her presence, or do enough for her. He became one with her in body and soul. His whole being was absorbed in her.

Through his love for Rebekah, "Isaac was comforted after his mother's death" (Gen. 24:67). The love of a man and a woman brings with it unexpected compensations. The leaving of family and cleaving to spouse as described in the creational ordering of marriage imply that a fulness of relationship will be achieved in the marriage union that satisfies all the basic social needs of the human being. This reality is not intended to discourage expanded social contacts among family and friends. But it indicates that all the basic human need for companionship will find a satisfactory provision in the marital union. This supplemental provision of marriage does not detract from but only complements the love of husband to wife and wife to husband.

From another perspective, it needs to be recognized that romantic love can be idolized. In his book *The Screwtape Letters*, C. S. Lewis depicts a demon as encouraging his underling to foil humans by promoting the false idea that "being in love" is "the only thing that makes marriage either happy or holy."[4] A romanticized idea of love can seriously mislead men and women alike. Furthermore, the perfecting of love must await the God-ordained process that makes the two into one after marriage. Nothing else can substitute for this long-term merging of body and soul in committed love. As with Isaac and Rebekah, it is often the case that the romance of love "follows the union rather than prompts it."[5]

But then, the romance of love that precedes marriage is an experience that can be equally real and true. In the case of Isaac, it is noted that he loved Rebekah after marriage. But in the case of Jacob's love for Rachel, it is stated that his extended time of service for the right of claiming her as his bride "seemed like only a few days to him because of his love for her" (Gen. 29:20). Before he was joined in marriage to her, for a period of seven long years Jacob had been madly in love with Rachel. This love continued after they were married (Gen. 29:30), but clearly true love existed before the two were wed.

So, a proper romantic love can come before or after marriage. But on the other hand, there can also be a wrong romantic love either before or after marriage. This cautionary word concerning romantic love must be noted well, particularly in light of modern abuses of the concept of falling in love. Love's attractions cannot ever be used as a justification for violating God's commandments that require a solemn life-commitment in conjunction with the privileges of marriage. Premarital or extramarital sexual relationships cannot be justified by an appeal to a person's "being in love" with someone outside the bonds of marriage, for those bonds involve a solemn oath for life.

Do you "love" someone other than the spouse to whom you are committed? Do you desire to have a sexual relationship with another? *Forget it!* It's of the devil, not of God. Scripture reports that King Solomon "loved many foreign women" (1 Kings 11:1).

God had indicated specifically that the Israelites must not intermarry with the peoples of the nations about them, because foreigners invariably would turn Israelite hearts to worshipping other gods. Yet Solomon "held fast in love" to his seven hundred wives of royal birth and his three hundred concubines (1 Kings 11:2c–3). He loved them, he clung to them, but he was altogether wrong in following the pulsations of love. The wisest man in the world got sorely, tragically confused over this matter of love's attractions. The consequences were disastrous. For "as Solomon grew old, his wives turned his heart after other gods, and his heart was not fully devoted to the LORD his God" (1 Kings. 11:4). In response to this deviation from divine law, the Lord became angry with Solomon and brought many adversaries against him.

Let all lesser men take note. If the wisest of humans can suffer from romantic illusions, who can presume that he will remain free from temptation and a fall? Beware of any romantic inclinations that contradict the orderings of the Word of God.

Still further, the occasional fading of romantic attractions must never be used as an excuse for neglecting the bonds of marriage that have been established. Scripture gives the unqualified command to husbands that they are to "love" their wives (Eph. 5:25). No appeal to the modern idea that a man may not be in love with his wife can nullify Scripture's commands. A man is to do acts of love toward his wife in every way possible, and it can be expected that feelings of love will follow.

In a similar way, older Christian women are given the responsibility of instructing younger women to "love" their husbands (Titus 2:4). Once more, the emphasis does not center first on nebulous feelings of love, but on the doing of love. Older women who have gone through the various phases of a marital relationship are the ones designated by God to communicate to less experienced younger women what it means to love their husbands through thick and thin, and how that love is to be expressed.

Have you ever been caught in a briar-patch? Have you ever hugged a sticker-bush? Some men are just like a briar-patch. Women must be taught how to love them. Clearly in these contexts the love of the marriage relationship is not presented purely in romantic terms. Instead, it is a matter primarily dealing with an unswerving commitment of one person to another.

Yet the reality of that thing called romantic love cannot be denied. In this relationship of one person to another may be found one of the most wondrous, most profound of mysteries in all God's creation. One author compares the distinctive quality of biblical prophecy to the mystery of human love:

> That quality is seen in the way love overtakes two people, brings them together, and binds them to each other, and in doing so scorns all institutions, all boundaries and conventions erected by men.[6]

Nothing can stop true love:

> For love is as strong as death.
> . . . .
> It burns like blazing fire,
> like a mighty flame.

Many waters cannot quench love;
>   rivers cannot wash it away.
If one were to give all the wealth of his house for love,
>   it would be utterly scorned. (Song of Songs 8:6–7)

Part of the profoundness of the Bible lies in its dealing realistically with all the various aspects of human life. The romance of love clearly is one of those areas in which extremes need to be rejected in favor of a good dose of sane reality. The biblical balance may serve as a healthy antidote to the many dangerously misleading misconceptions of today. Love is indeed a wondrous thing, a special design of the Creator in which he continues to be intimately involved in the lives of the people he has made. The romantic dimension of love continues to have a vital role to play as a marriage stretches across the years. At the same time, the deeper commitments of fidelity that serve as the underlying foundation for a marital union must never be forgotten.

■ ■ ■ ■ ■

THE CONSEQUENCES OF MARRIAGE CHOICES

Pharaoh gave Joseph . . . Asenath daughter of Potiphera,
priest of On, to be his wife. —Genesis 41:45

Often people have the idea that romantic entanglement is a private affair with little or no societal significance. They think that their relationship affects no one but themselves. So they conclude it is nobody else's business. But love and marriage always have far-reaching consequences that go well beyond the two principal parties. Not only for families and friends, but for generations to come, a love relationship has significant impact on the lives of others.

Esau chose to marry Canaanite women, which caused great grief to the hearts of Isaac and Rebekah, his father and mother (Gen. 26:34–35). When he finally understood that his Canaanite wives were a grief to his parents, he proceeded to take as a third wife a descendant of Ishmael, the son of Abraham by Hagar the Egyptian (Gen. 28:8–9). No doubt this taking of an additional wife did little to alleviate the grief of Isaac and Rebekah.

In any case, Esau quickly develops a large family, too large to allow him to continue in the same territory with his brother Jacob (Gen. 36:6–8). As a consequence, he eventually settles in the land of Seir, among the rugged mountains to the southeast of the Dead Sea. Esau ends up outside the land of promise, separated from the chosen seed.

Marriage brings with it far-reaching consequences. By being joined to people of another religious commitment, Esau separated himself and his descendants from the blessings of God's promise of redemption.

Yet these negative consequences of a "bad" marriage are not totally irreversible. God in the bounties of his grace delights to reach into hopeless situations and work savingly. Eventually God's name is placed on the Edomite descendants of Esau, indicating that God's electing grace has been directed to the line of

Esau just as it had been to the line of Jacob (Amos 9:12; cf. Deut. 28:9–10).

Marriage can have an effect on position in society as well as in the realm of redemption. Part of the pharaoh's exaltation of Joseph was the marriage arrangement made for him. In addition to making Joseph second-in-command of the whole land of Egypt, the pharaoh gave him Asenath daughter of the priest of On to be his wife (Gen. 41:43, 45). As has been pointed out, even the pharaohs of Egypt "chose their wives out of this family," providing a further indication of the honor being accorded Joseph.[7] He was being given the privilege of marrying "the daughter of a priest of the sun, the most distinguished caste in the land."[8] In this newfound position of honor, Joseph "went throughout the land of Egypt," and no doubt was received royally by the whole of Egyptian society, partly because of the prominence that came through association with his new bride (Gen. 41:45c).

Marriage motivated primarily for reasons of social status can be disastrous. Yet the fact must be recognized: marriage choices have clear consequences socially that must be lived with for a long time. Of course, love's choices may determine to eschew all considerations of societal honor. Such decisions should not be despised, but recognized as a witness to the power of human love. It may be that those who marry merely to attain positions of honor or wealth are the ones who ought to be pitied the most.

■ ■ ■ ■ ■

THE LOVE-TRIANGLE

I have had a great struggle with my sister,
and I have won. —Genesis 30:8

The intimacies of the marriage relationship are of such a vitally personal nature that the intrusion of a third person into the scene invariably leads to the most intense manifestations of resentment to be found anywhere in human experience. Volumes have been written recounting the jealousies, the intrigues, the hatred, murder, and bad blood that has flowed as a consequence of a love-triangle. One of the most quotable quotes in recent years came from the lips of a prominent athlete accused of bludgeoning his ex-wife and her new boyfriend. He said in effect, "If I did what they say I did, doesn't that show how much I loved her?" Despite the persistent efforts of mankind in every generation and culture to circumvent the creational orderings, sex is meant for two and only two. Consider two examples in Genesis of the tragic developments arising from a failure to respect the limitations of the marriage order as established by God at creation.

For years Abraham and Sarah could have no children. Sarah passed the age at which it would be possible, humanly speaking, for her to conceive. Presuming to herself the responsibility of fulfilling God's promise to her husband concerning his multitudinous seed, Sarah proposed that she provide for him a surrogate wife who could bear children for him. In this way, Sarah hoped to "build a family through her" (Gen. 16:2). So in this case, the love-triangle was created by the wife herself.

As Sarah had proposed, Abraham had a son by her handmaid Hagar. It would seem that all her plans had succeeded, and that she should have been quite satisfied with the results.

But the sensitivities of the human soul are not easily suppressed. In a typical manifestation of the frustrations that invariably accompany the jealousies of a spouse, Sarah turns her ire on her husband Abraham. "You are responsible for the wrong I am suffering," she says (Gen. 16:5). Even though the whole relationship was initiated by Sarah herself (Gen. 16:2–3), she now blames Abraham for her misery. All the peace of the happy household has been shattered.

Hagar's own reaction to her pregnancy also follows exactly the line of development that might have been anticipated. As soon as she determines that she is pregnant, she proudly flaunts her new-found status and begins to despise her mistress (Gen. 16:4b). Sarah has had her chance over the past decade. Now Hagar will prove the real worth of a woman. What is Sarah now that Hagar is the one to bear a son for Abraham? So the love-triangle inevitably breeds strife, jealousy, dissension, pride, and trouble in every direction.

Evidence supporting this same perspective in Genesis may be drawn from the account of the love-triangle formed by Jacob and his two wives Leah and Rachel (Gen. 29:31–30:24). Leah has six sons before Rachel has had a single child. To compensate for her barrenness, Rachel presents Jacob with her handmaid. But then Leah, in order to remain on top of this struggle between Jacob's wives, responds by doing the same. Eventually Rachel also bears Jacob a son. She names him Joseph, which means "May God add."

Not at all content with one son, Rachel memorializes her desire for more sons with the naming of her first. She eventually has her prayer answered with the birth of Benjamin, but pays dearly for this second son with her own life at childbirth (Gen. 35:16–18).

Obviously the two women are vying for the affection of the one man who is husband to them both. When Rachel's handmaid produces a second son on her behalf, she exclaims, "I have had a great struggle with my sister, and I have won" (Gen. 30:8). Literally the text reads "I have struggled greatly before God," which is a Hebraic way of saying, "I have had a massive struggle."9 Throughout their lives these two sisters agonize in their jealous striving with one another.

Jacob ends up with twelve sons, but also with a clearly defined rift within the family. This division formed by the rivalry between children of two different wives eventually breaks out in the murderous jealousy of the sons of Leah against the favored son of Rachel. A young, naive Joseph taunts his brothers by spelling out his superiority as revealed in his dreams. Even his father and mother will bow to him. His half-brothers hate him so much that they cannot even speak a kind word to him (Gen. 37:4). Eventually the brothers seize an opportunity first to plot Joseph's murder, but then to sell him into slavery. Jacob shows no awareness of the problem created by his favoritism toward the children of his favored wife, and redirects the discriminatory love he had shown Joseph toward Rachel's younger son Benjamin (Gen. 42:38). It all develops out of the tragic failure to be unswervingly committed to the one spouse of God's providential choice.

In many nations today, the law forbids having more than one

wife at the same time. But the principle behind this law is violated constantly. The ease with which divorce can be attained has fostered a virtual institution which may be designated as "sequential polygamy." It is assumed that by a legal divorce peace, harmony, and happiness may be maintained among people involved in the seemingly inevitable love-triangle.

But that will never be the case. The love-triangle can only bring unhappiness, heartache, strife, contention, jealousy, hatred, murder, and devastated lives. From the beginning it has been God's intent to have only two people joined in the intimacies of love. His fullest blessing will rest only on those who live according to his design.

■ ■ ■ ■ ■

THE MARRIAGE OF BELIEVER TO UNBELIEVER

The sons of God saw that the daughters of men were beautiful, and they married any of them they chose. —Genesis 6:2

As the wickedness of man increased on the earth, the "sons of God" saw that the "daughters of men" were beautiful, and they married any of them they chose (Gen. 6: 1–2). Who were these "sons of God," and what is the significance of their marriage to the "daughters of men"?

Four views stand out among the many interpretations that have been given to this passage. The first option proposes that supernatural beings, possibly creatures from another world, co-habited with humans, causing the birth of an offspring of giants. One modern translation interprets the passage so that it reads:

> Some of the supernatural beings saw that these girls were beautiful, so they took the ones they liked. . . . In those days, and even later, there were giants on the earth who were descendants of human women and the supernatural beings. (Gen. 6:2, 4)[10]

This rather bizarre analysis stretches the language of the text quite severely, and is essentially unworthy of Scripture. No evidence can be found in the Bible to support the view either that creatures exist in another world, or that they would be capable of intermarrying with humans so as to produce offspring.[11]

Secondly, these "sons of God" are understood to be angels. This interpretation makes better sense in view of the fact that the phrase "sons of God" elsewhere in the Old Testament can refer to angels (Job 1:6; 2:1; 38:7; and possibly Dan. 3:25).[12] But from the biblical context it is by no means clear that the passage intends to indicate that gods or angels cohabited with humans.[13] For the equivalent of the phrase "sons of God" is used in a number of passages to indicate something other than supernatural beings. The term "sons" is used to designate the godly seed (Ps. 73:15; Deut. 32:5; Hos. 1:10).

Conclusively telling against the view that these "sons of God" were angels is the testimony of Jesus himself that angels neither marry nor are given in marriage (Matt. 22:30; Mark. 12:25; cf.

Luke. 20:34–36).[14] No adequate reason exists to attribute the uniqueness of the offspring of these marriages to cohabitation with angels.

Thirdly, the "sons of God" have been identified as kings. This interpretation reflects the dignity of the title "sons of God." According to one interpreter, this designation refers both to divine beings and to "ancient rulers of the pre-Flood world who were regarded as divine or semi-divine."[15] But it is doubtful that the phrase is used this way elsewhere in the Bible. At the same time, the concept of all the redeemed as being the sons of God is a theme that runs throughout the Scriptures.

Fourthly, it is proposed that the phrase "sons of God" refers to the "seed of the woman" that would enter into conflict with Satan, in accordance with the first messianic promise of Scripture (cf. Gen. 3:15). This godly seed would stand in contrast to the "daughters of men," representing the natural offspring of sinful humanity apart from the redeeming grace of God. This classic interpretation fits best the broader Genesis context, in which the two "seeds" are being developed in contrast to one another.[16]

The tragedy of the event is seen in the fact that the "seed of God" is being united with the "seed of Satan." The consequences of this sad story are told over and over again throughout human history. This first instance of the sons of God marrying the daughters of men contributes to a wickedness in the heart of man that is so great that "every imagination of the thoughts of his heart" is only evil all the day (Gen. 6:5*). Eventually God determines that he must wipe man from the face of the earth by the flood.

If there remains any question about the wrongness in God's

eyes of a believer marrying an unbeliever, consider the explicit teaching of several passages of Scripture:

First, Exodus 34:15–16:

> Be careful not to make a treaty with those who live in the land; for when they prostitute themselves to their gods and sacrifice to them, they will invite you and you will eat their sacrifices. And *when you choose some of their daughters as wives for your sons and those daughters prostitute themselves to their gods, they will lead your sons to do the same.*

Everyone has a god. If a person's god is not being formally worshipped, it may be even more dangerous to a worshipper of the true God because of its subtlety. A spouse who worships another god will gradually draw his or her partner from wholehearted commitment to God's work. In addition, when children are born to the marriage, it is impossible for a non-Christian spouse to teach the child to pray properly, or to read the Bible with faith, or to trust in Jesus as the Christ. Children will follow their father's religion just as naturally as they follow their father's footsteps. They will drink their mother's religion just as naturally as they feed on their mother's milk.

Secondly, Deuteronomy 7:3–4:

> Do not intermarry with them. Do not give your daughters to their sons or take their daughters for your sons, for they will turn your sons away from following me to serve other gods, and the LORD's anger will burn against you and will quickly destroy you.

The Lord unequivocally commands it. Do not intermarry with unbelievers.

Two reasons are given for the prohibition in this passage. First, do not intermarry with unbelievers because they will turn your descendants away from following the Lord. In other words, they will lead the future generations of the people of God into a life of sin. Secondly, do not intermarry with unbelievers because the Lord's anger will burn against you and will quickly destroy you. The people of God should need no further reason. To avoid the anger of the Lord, do not marry the unbeliever.

Thirdly, Judges 3:4, 6:

> [The Canaanites] were left to test the Israelites to see whether they would obey the LORD's commands, which he had given their forefathers through Moses. . . . They took their daughters in marriage and gave their own daughters to their sons, and served their gods.

God lets his people live among unbelievers for two reasons. First, he wants the believer to be a witness to the unbeliever; and secondly, he tests the believer to see if he will obey his commands. Among the Lord's commands is the instruction that the believer must not marry the unbeliever.

Men and women who are unbelievers can be kind, loving, considerate, handsome, beautiful, and attractive. The prophet Ezekiel describes the nation of Israel as lusting after her lovers, the Assyrians—"warriors clothed in blue, governors and commanders, all of them handsome young men and mounted horsemen" (Ezek. 23:5–6). But the people of God must not be deceived. The person standing on a chair invariably will be pulled down by the person whose feet are firmly planted on the ground. The person who marries an unbelieving spouse can very easily be pulled down to the other person's level, just as the Israelites who intermarried with idol-worshippers eventually worshipped idols themselves.

Fourthly, 1 Kings 11:1–11:

King Solomon . . . loved many foreign women besides Pharaoh's daughter—Moabites, Ammonites, Edomites, Sidonians and Hittites. They were from nations about which the LORD had told the Israelites, "You must not intermarry with them, because they will surely turn your hearts after their gods." Nevertheless, Solomon held fast to them in love. He had seven hundred wives of royal birth and three hundred concubines, and his wives led him astray. As Solomon grew old, his wives turned his heart after other gods, and his heart was not fully devoted to the LORD his God, as the heart of David his father had been. He followed Ashtoreth the goddess of the Sidonians, and Molech the detestable god of the Ammonites. So Solomon did evil in the eyes of the LORD; he did not follow the LORD completely, as David his father had done.

On a hill east of Jerusalem, Solomon built a high place for Chemosh the detestable god of Moab, and for Molech the detestable god of the Ammonites. He did the same for all his foreign wives, who burned incense and offered sacrifices to their gods.

The LORD became angry with Solomon because his heart had turned away from the LORD, the God of Israel, who had appeared to him twice. Although he had forbidden Solomon to follow other gods, Solomon did not keep the LORD's command. So the LORD said to Solomon, "Since this is your attitude and you have not kept my covenant and my decrees, which I commanded you, I will most certainly tear the kingdom away from you and give it to one of your subordinates. . . ."

Some people may be tempted to think they are wiser than the Israelites, that they can overcome the tendency to be unduly influenced by an unbelieving spouse. Anyone thinking along those lines should consider the fate of the wisest man who ever lived on the face of the earth (other than Jesus Christ). Consider the effect of intermarriage with unbelievers on King Solomon.

Not while he was young, but "as Solomon grew old," his wives turned him toward other gods, and his heart was not fully devoted to the Lord (v. 4). It might be supposed that wisdom would increase with age. But in the case of a relationship with an unbelieving spouse, the truth is just the opposite. Just across from Jerusalem's temple mount at the place that came to be known as the "hill of abominations," Solomon built multiple temples for the foreign gods of his various wives. As a consequence, the Lord became angry, and divided his kingdom.

Consider carefully the consequence of Solomon's sin. For the next two hundred years the divided kingdom of God's people warred against itself. The identical thing can happen among God's people today. Intermarriage of believers with unbelievers brings strife not only in the home, but also in the realms of church and state.

If a person is tempted to rationalize by thinking that this prohibition applied only to people of the old covenant era, consider, fifthly, the teaching of Paul in 2 Corinthians 6:14–18:

Do not be yoked together with unbelievers. For what do righteousness and wickedness have in common? Or what fellowship can light have with darkness? What harmony is there between Christ and Belial? What does a believer have in common with an unbeliever? What agreement is there between the temple of God and idols? For we are the temple of the living God. As God has said: "I will live with them and walk among them, and I will be their God, and they will be my people."

"Therefore come out from them
   and be separate,
      says the Lord.
Touch no unclean thing,
   and I will receive you."
"I will be a Father to you,
   and you will be my sons and daughters,
      says the Lord Almighty."

Worse than Solomon's providing temples for foreign gods across the valley from the temple of the Lord is the believer's joining his body, which is the temple of the Holy Spirit, to the body and spirit of a person worshipping other gods. For then the worship of foreign gods has been introduced into the Most Holy Place of the Lord, the place where he abides.

The teaching of Scripture is unmistakable. The believer in Christ is not to marry the unbeliever. Yet constantly God's people are tempted to compromise the standard of holiness. The natural desire to be married leads people to rationalize a relationship in any number of ways. This other person is kind and considerate despite his lack of saving faith. Or the attractions of "love" are too strong to be ignored. Or the prospective partner is "so open" to listening to the gospel.

But eventually the bonding of the redeemed seed of God with the unredeemed seed of Satan must result in sadness, frustration, disappointment, and often tragedy. In cases in which a believer is drawn to the prospect of marriage to an unbeliever, it is not a matter of determining exactly what may be the will of God. For God has made quite plain his will. The Christian is not to be unequally yoked together with the non-Christian.

■ ■ ■ ■ ■

THE MISMATCHED MARRIAGE

Esau . . . married Judith daughter of Beeri the Hittite, and also
Basemath daughter of Elon the Hittite. They were a source of
grief to Isaac and Rebekah. —Genesis 26:34–35

One of the most dreaded circumstances imaginable in life is the mismatched marriage. Some people are terrified about the prospect of marriage just because they fear the possibility of being wed forever to the "wrong" person.

Undoubtedly some people end up in what would appear to be a mismatched marriage. Yet great care must be taken in reaching this conclusion about a marriage union. People may use the idea of a mismatched marriage as an excuse for despairing over their future, or for limiting their service to Christ, or for wrongly filing for divorce. As a matter of fact, great divergences of personality, education, culture, or mood may be overcome in the marriage relationship, if only people are patient, faithful, and trusting in God. Never is there reason to despair over a relationship in marriage.

Elizabeth Goudge the English novelist tells an intriguing story of two sisters who had an interest in the same man.[17] The older sister was convinced that she was the object of his affection. But he actually loved her younger sister. The man sailed from the English Channel Islands to New Zealand, and some years later wrote to the father of the two sisters, proposing marriage and asking that the father allow his chosen bride to sail out to meet him. After several months of waiting, the man stood at the dock, eagerly watching to catch the first glimpse of his beloved. But down the gangplank came . . . the wrong sister. The names of the two sisters were somewhat similar, the man had been drinking when he penned the letter of proposal, and he had scribbled the wrong name!

What was he to do? In an air of possessive triumph, the older sister was fast approaching. In this moment of desperation, the man hid his face in a lengthy embrace. He then proceeded to marry her. For years afterward the mismatched couple had a stormy relationship.

Near the end of their lives, the couple returned home to the Channel Islands. By this time, the younger sister had entered a convent. Through an inadvertent remark, the man revealed to his wife that the younger sister actually had been the object of his love.

In an uncharacteristically unselfish fashion, the older sister humbled herself and made known to her younger sister that she had been the chosen one. This generous action had the effect of breaking down the barrier that had existed between husband and wife through all the years of their marriage. From that point on they learned how to love one another genuinely. Once this dramatic change in their relationship had been experienced, the seemingly mismatched marriage proved to be something quite different.

Though the novel is fiction, the story is factual, and the lesson is clear. Virtually any marriage can work, so long as people are willing to surrender personal preferences for the greater good of a stable relationship.

The one circumstance that can cause the greatest root-problem in a marriage relationship is the union of a person in covenant with God to a person that is not in the same covenant relationship. For if the proper basis for a reconciliation with God through the personal experience of forgiveness of sins is lacking, then an adequate basis for reconciliation between marriage partners in the event of a disharmonious relationship will not be found. Misunderstandings and offenses between husband and wife are bound to arise, and a proper grasp of the way of reconciliation as revealed in God's giving up his Son for the redemption of sinners provides the only effective way to the reestablishment of a fully harmonious relationship. If two are not agreed at this most basic point, they will find it extremely difficult to walk together.

The matter of a mismatched marriage finds vivid illustration in the case of Isaac's son Esau. Esau was forty years of age when he married, the same age his father Isaac had been when he married Esau's mother Rebekah (Gen. 26:34; 25:20). Perhaps in his own way Esau was attempting to emulate the example of his revered father. But whatever his motives may have been, Esau seems to have had great trouble grasping the basic principle behind his father's earlier choice of a bride. For instead of marrying someone who presumably would have the same faith-commitment as his father, Esau married two Hittite women (Gen. 26:34). The reason for regarding these unions as mismatched marriages is not based on a racial distinction, but on a religious distinction. It may be assumed that Esau's Hittite wives did not worship the God that had revealed himself to Abraham and Isaac. These two Hittite wives of Esau "were a source of grief to Isaac and Rebekah" (Gen. 26:35). Not only did Esau create a circumstance that guaranteed trouble for himself by marrying women with a different religious orientation; he was also assured of trouble by marrying two wives rather than one.

Esau's total misconception along these lines becomes obvious in a subsequent development. His mother, Rebekah, expresses herself rather explicitly to her husband Isaac on this matter. She is "disgusted" with life itself because of the Hittite women that surround her darling Jacob. If her favored son should marry one of these women, she asserts, then life would not be worth living (Gen. 27:46). In response to her concerns, Isaac admonishes Jacob not to marry a Canaanite woman (as Esau had done), and sends him away to find a wife among his relatives (Gen. 28:1–2).

In his own misguided way, Esau actually attempts to please his parents. When he hears that Jacob has been sent away to find a wife taken from their relatives, he finally realizes how displeasing his Canaanite wives must be to his parents. So to "remedy" the situation he proceeds to marry Mahalath the daughter of Ishmael, the son of Abraham by Hagar the Egyptian (Gen. 28:6–9).

Esau simply could not get it right. By taking to himself a third wife, he only compounded the problem. The addition of a wife that was a descendant from Abraham could not alleviate his marital difficulties. Only the grace of God could make right the deep-seated problems caused by Esau's lack of a proper faith in God that could reconcile him to God and men.

Happily the later testimonies of Scripture indicate just how wondrously the grace of God can redeem any human situation no matter how complex. For the prophet Amos anticipates the day in which Edom, embodying the descendants of Esau's three wives, shall have God's name placed on them, indicating that they are to become the elect children of God (Amos 9:12; cf. Deut. 28:9–10, where the identical phrase is applied to God's election of Israel).

All the loving favors that come to the sons and daughters of God will belong to the descendants of Esau. It is this very Scripture from Amos that ultimately becomes the basis for the inclusion of the multitudes of gentile peoples that were swarming into the family of God under the blessings of the new covenant (Acts 15:15–19). Without a drop of Abrahamic blood running through their veins and despite all the irregularities of marital relationships that characterize the gentile world, masses can be brought into the fulness of God's blessing along with believing Jews (Eph. 2:19; 3:6).

In this regard, the explicit instruction given to Christian believers who find themselves married to unbelievers should be noted well. This circumstance of a mismatched marriage might occur when one member of a non-Christian couple is converted while the other is not. Or it might be brought about by a Christian's marrying a person that does not profess Christ despite the clear prohibition of Scripture against such unions. Or it might occur by a non-Christian's deceiving a Christian, professing to be a believer, but showing his true colors only after marriage. In any of these circumstances, the basic principles remain the same.

If the unbelieving spouse departs, canceling the marital relationship, then the believer should let him depart (1 Cor. 7:15). In such circumstances, the believing spouse is not bound. A divorce has occurred that is recognized by God as canceling the marital obligations of the innocent party, which gives the believer freedom to marry again.

But so long as the unbeliever wishes to remain married to the believer, then the believer must not divorce the unbelieving spouse (1 Cor. 7:12–13). Why? The believer should remain married to the unbeliever under these circumstances because the real possibility exists that the unbeliever will be brought to faith by the testimony of the believer (1 Cor. 7:16; cf. 1 Peter 3:1–2).

How great is the grace of God in its rich manifestations to a sinful, often misled human race! No matter what a person's marital situation may be, he has reason for hope. The most mismatched of marriages may find a blessed reconciliation and harmonization through the grace that is in Jesus Christ.

■ ■ ■ ■ ■

UNREQUITED LOVE

The LORD saw that Leah was not loved. —Genesis 29:31

One of the most difficult circumstances in this life is for a person to love though not being loved in return. It is not easy to explain how or why such situations arise, but they are nonetheless very real to the person involved. Not only outside marriage, but within the formal bonds of marriage, love often is unrequited. Perhaps a couple begins with love enough. But somewhere, somehow the spark of love dies in the soul of one or the other in the marital relationship. How painful in those circumstances it must be to love but not to be loved in return!

Leah was brought into this situation through the connivings of her father Laban. Jacob the tall, dark stranger from a far country obviously was in love with Leah's younger, more beautiful sister Rachel. For seven years he worked for his future father-in-law to earn the privilege of marrying Rachel. The wedding ceremony went off as planned, and Jacob took his bride into the wedding tent. Not until the next morning did the light of day uncover the fact that he actually had been wed to Leah, the older of the two sisters (Gen. 29:16–26).

The frustration of Jacob has been well recorded, and can be fully understood. But little has been said about the humiliation that Leah must have experienced. What were her thoughts, her agonies, as she was substituted as a "pseudo-bride" in place of her sister? How did she react to Jacob's deep disappointment over her on the morning after their wedding? She may have developed some natural affection for Jacob, but nothing indicates that Jacob had a care about her.

Leah responds to this very painful situation by striving, reaching out in the only way she can to win the love and respect that have been denied her. She will honor her husband by presenting him with many children. Actually it is God himself who arranges for this compensation. As the Scripture notes: "When the LORD saw that Leah was not loved, he opened her womb, but Rachel was barren" (Gen. 29:31). This special grace of the Lord may be understood as God's compensatory gift to Leah.

The lesson should not be forgotten. The omniscient God sees every little slight of his children, and has his ways of alleviating their pain. A person who may not feel properly loved should be encouraged to look around and see how God may be making up for this lack in life.

When she has borne her first son, Leah exclaims: "It is because the LORD has seen my misery. Surely my husband will love me now" (Gen. 29:32). With a truly perceptive faith, she understands the secret workings of the Lord. But she cannot be satisfied until she has won the heart of her husband. Yet she is destined to bear her pain for many more years. Her wounded heart expresses itself on the occasion of giving birth to her next two sons:

Because the LORD heard that I am not loved, he gave me this one too. (Gen. 29:33)

Now at last my husband will become attached to me, because I have borne him three sons. (Gen. 29:34)

Finally Leah reaches some level of reconciliation with her situation. For with the birth of her fourth son, she says simply: "This time I will praise the LORD" (Gen. 29:35). She has not seen a change in her husband's affections. But she determines that she will center her attention on the goodness of God.

Yet the sense of injustice in the failure of her husband to love her must have run deeply in the soul of Leah. For when Rachel asks her to share some of her son Reuben's mandrakes, Leah shows just how strongly she feels. According to one commentator, it was believed in ancient times that this fruit "was a stimulant to sexual desire or served as an aphrodisiac. Some prepared a drink from the fruit, which was considered to be a love potion."[18] Apparently in the days of the patriarchs, the mandrake was used "as a means of promoting child-bearing."[19] So in effect, Rachel the barren "rival wife" is asking Leah to provide her with the means to become fertile. Leah explodes: "Wasn't it enough that you took away my husband? Will you take my son's mandrakes too?" (Gen. 30:15). All these years Leah has harbored this resentment against her sister. Interestingly it is always Leah, never Rachel, who designates Jacob as "my husband" (Gen. 29:32, 34; 30:15, 18, 20). Even though she had surreptitiously claimed Jacob as her own husband on the occasion that should have been Rachel's wedding night, Leah felt she had been justified by the custom of the day. For tradition required that the oldest daughter be married first. In that light, Leah has concluded that Rachel should have backed off rather than insisting on her own claim to Jacob.

Rachel seeks to mollify her sister's ire as well as to promote her own fertility by proposing to grant to Leah, who apparently has been neglected by Jacob for some time (perhaps even years), a claim to Jacob as her husband for the night in exchange for some of Reuben's mandrakes. Leah agrees to the arrangement, and informs Jacob of his obligation when he returns from the field in the evening.

God hears the heartbroken cry of unloved Leah, and she bears two more sons to Jacob. In response to the birth of the last of her sons she declares, "God has presented me with a precious gift. This time my husband will treat me with honor, because I have borne him six sons" (Gen. 30:20). Now it seems that she finally has given up on thinking that somehow she will turn Jacob's affection toward her. She will be satisfied if only he will give her the honor she deserves for presenting him with no fewer than six sons.

Unrequited love is a reality that must be faced by many people. This heartrending situation may extend across the years, and never be resolved with any satisfaction. Leah must be commended for displaying a faith that continued to look to the Lord in her distress. Even though she showed her resentment toward her sister in a very human response, she nonetheless persisted in crying out to the Lord and acknowledging his gracious help. Little more can be expected of God's people who suffer from unrequited love in any generation.

■ ■ ■ ■ ■

THE FAMILY CONNECTION

Then Rachel and Leah replied, "Do we still have any share in the inheritance of our father's estate? Does he not regard us as foreigners? . . . So do whatever God has told you."
—Genesis 31:14–16

Paramount among human relationships is the bond between parents and children. The natural connection created between a father and mother as they bring a child into the world is reinforced by parental care that extends over the most formative years of a young person's life.

But something happens at marriage. The Genesis description of the strong bond created by marriage may be understood quite legitimately as a statement of fact as well as a command. A man shall leave his father and mother (this severance of persons happens at marriage) and shall cleave to his wife (this union of persons also happens at the marriage), and the two shall be one flesh (this mysterious blending of persons explains the depth of the union). In any number of ways people may attempt to deny the reality of these happenings at marriage, but they are nonetheless a part of marital union. Indeed, the obligation to honor parents continues throughout life. But upon marriage a new priority is set. Efforts to violate this priority can only bring confusion and tensions into the bonds of marriage as well as into the bonds of parent-child relations.

For twenty years Jacob lived in the household of Laban. During this time, Laban's daughters became Jacob's wives, and their children were Laban's grandchildren. But the time came when Jacob felt he must break the ties with Laban and return to his own land. He had suffered many abuses from his father-in-law as a consequence of their business relationships, and he felt compelled to strike out on his own.

What would Laban's daughters do? How would they respond to this challenge to their loyalties to parents? The text of Genesis leaves no doubt regarding their sense of priority:

> Then Rachel and Leah replied, "Do we still have any share in the inheritance of our father's estate? Does he not regard us as foreigners? . . . And has he not eaten up our silver?[20] . . . So do whatever God has told you." (Gen. 31:14–16*)

The words of Jacob's wives make plain the fact that a new family unit has been created by their marriage. Their loyalty of family connection now resides with the new union that has been established. Both Leah and Rachel manifest unswerving commitment to their spouse.

Strengthened in his resolve by the assent of his wives, Jacob made good his plan to leave the household of his father-in-law without notice. He was certain that Laban would create trouble if he made known his intention to leave. No doubt Laban would have reacted exactly as Jacob had anticipated, had it not been for God's direct warning to Laban in a dream (Gen. 31:24).

Laban overtakes his fleeing family and rebukes them for their abrupt departure.[21] Jacob retorts by noting the mistreatment he has endured for the past twenty years. The two finally reach an agreement. Jacob will not take any other women as his wives, and Laban will not cross borders to harm Jacob. Laban then kisses his grandchildren and daughters, blesses them and departs (Gen. 31:55).

The responsibilities to a new family unit established by marriage supersede all previous commitments. This fact needs to be realized as a basic consequence of marriage. Indeed, it needs to be recognized that a person marries into a family and not just an individual. Yet parents no longer will play the major role in the life of either partner. A new family connection has been established that takes on larger proportions than previous relationships, no matter how significant they may have been.

■ ■ ■ ■ ■

DIVORCE

Abraham . . . sent [Hagar] off with the boy. —Genesis 21:14

Nothing quite like modern divorce is found in the book of Genesis. Yet the circumstances surrounding the separation of

Hagar from Abraham may serve to illuminate the many difficulties that accompany divorce.

It was at the instigation of Sarah, Abraham's wife, that the patriarch took to himself Sarah's handmaid Hagar as a wife (Gen. 16:1–4). This arrangement suited exactly the Mesopotamian custom of the day.[22] By providing a slave-girl to her husband for the purposes of childbearing, Sarah prevented Abraham from taking a concubine on his own. But her efforts resulted only in compounding rather than resolving the problem of an heir. By following the devices of her own heart rather than continuing to trust the Lord in this admittedly difficult circumstance, Sarah succeeded only in multiplying the dissension in her household. Although the custom prevalent in the culture of the day allowed Abraham to take Hagar to himself, God did not approve it. The same situation so often prevails in the matter of divorce today. Human custom allows it, but God does not approve it, except in very specific circumstances.

It was also the initiative of Sarah that brought about the separation of Hagar from the family. Sarah could not endure the arrogance of her own handmaid, who was now pregnant by her husband. Although the narrative of Scripture is quite brief in its record of the interchange between Sarah and Abraham on this point, it would seem very likely that the dialogue (or monologue) stretched over a good period of time. The pillow-talk of Sarah with (or to) her husband must not have been very pleasant during those days. Just a few snippets of her recorded remarks (Gen. 16:5) suffice to give an understanding of the point she was making:

"You are responsible for the wrong I am suffering!"

"I put my servant in your arms, and now . . . she despises me!"

"May the LORD judge between you and me!"

As has been well noted, even the best-ordered families are sometimes not free from contentions.[23]

Abraham had a domestic difficulty that he could not resolve. Possibly as he was turning over in his bed seeking sleep, he could be overheard mumbling to his disgruntled spouse: "Your servant is in your hands. . . . Do with her whatever you think best" (Gen. 16:6).

Sarah's best thoughts were to do whatever was necessary to drive the intruder out of her household. So the "divorce" of Abraham from Hagar, if it may be so called, was initiated by Sarah. She could not stand having an expectant rival-mate living with her beloved, and so she made Hagar so uncomfortable that she fled to find relief.

The formal context of divorce in the modern day is quite different. But often a similar set of dynamics is at work. A married man or woman develops a relationship with a third party. Over a matter of time, someone in the relationship concludes that he/she cannot abide the prevailing circumstance. So divorce is inevitable.

It should be recognized that according to the teaching of Jesus, the innocent party of a marriage into which a third party has been improperly introduced possesses a God-sanctioned right to divorce

(Matt. 19:9). It would be quite appropriate for ministers involved in premarital counseling to point out to each prospective couple that a person forfeits every right involved in a marriage relationship if he or she acts in infidelity to the spouse. The person that has remained faithful to the marriage commitments should not be compelled to seek relief through divorce, but the right is nonetheless present. If a divorce on proper biblical grounds has in fact been finalized, the person that has remained faithful to the marriage vows is then free to remarry.

But divorce wrongly sought only compounds problems. Sarah treats Hagar so badly that the poor woman flees into the desert. In her desperate circumstance, the Lord appears to her, gives her reassurance concerning her son, and directs her to return and live in submission to Sarah (Gen. 16:7–10).

Although Hagar returned as directed by the Lord, eventually she and her son are sent away permanently. When Isaac is born to Abraham and Sarah as the child designated to inherit the covenantal blessings, a bitter rivalry springs up. At the time of the weaning of Isaac, which most probably was celebrated because it meant the child had survived the high mortality rate prevalent at the time, Hagar's son Ishmael was found "mocking" the defenseless toddler (Gen. 21:9). At this point Sarah can stand no more. She insists that Abraham send away Hagar and her son. Though in great distress, Abraham does what Sarah asks, but only after God has assented to the dismissal, and promised to bless this son as well as Isaac (Gen. 21:8–13).

Given certain circumstances delineated in Scripture, divorce may be appropriate though not desirable (Matt. 19:9; 1 Cor. 7:15).

But almost invariably it creates tension and trouble that last across the generations. The Creator who ordained marriage finds no pleasure in its improper dissolution. As the Lord has said in the most explicit terms, "I hate divorce" (Mal. 2:16).

Accepting this teaching regarding the impropriety of divorce may be particularly difficult to people in the modern circumstance, when divorce is so common. Yet Jesus plainly taught that the person who divorces his spouse for any reason other than marital infidelity, and marries another, has committed adultery (Matt. 19:9). Many sins may be involved in a divorce, including the violation of vows taken before God and the neglect of responsibility to lovingly care for one's spouse. But Jesus focuses on the adultery involved in remarriage after an improper divorce, which is based on the understanding that God who has joined a couple does not recognize the human separation as an actual divorce.

This teaching was equally difficult in Jesus' own day, as is seen by his disciples' response: "If this is the situation between a husband and wife, it is better not to marry" (Matt. 19:10). Yet Jesus refuses to compromise his position despite the dismay of his disciples. He acknowledges that indeed some people will end up not marrying. But in the case of those who do marry, it must be recognized that what God has joined together no man is to put asunder. Anyone, man or woman, who divorces a spouse, except for the cause of marital infidelity, and marries another, commits adultery (Matt. 19:9; Mark. 10:9–12).

God in the richness of his grace may bless people with fulness of life despite the fact that they have gone through a divorce. They may have to live with some of the consequences of a marital separation. But even as God placed his benediction on Hagar, Ishmael, and Abraham, so he can pour out his grace on the life of the divorced and their offspring.

■ ■ ■ ■ ■

THE SECOND MARRIAGE

Abraham took another wife, whose name was Keturah.
—Genesis 25:1

After many years of being happily married, death parts Abraham and Sarah. The beloved wife of Abraham died at the age of a hundred and twenty-seven years (Gen. 23:1). At her death, Abraham mourned and wept over the loss of his beloved life partner.

Abraham lived until he was a hundred and seventy-five (Gen. 25:7). Since Sarah was ten years younger than Abraham (Gen. 17:17), it may be deduced that Abraham lived approximately forty years beyond Sarah's death, which would involve about a quarter of his adult life.

Scripture reports that Abraham took another wife named Keturah, who bore the patriarch six sons (Gen. 25:1). As any two people will be quite different in virtually every way, so the person who marries a second time may expect that life with a different partner will be quite different. The way of dressing will be different, the expectations concerning order in the home will be different, as will the established schedules of rising in the morning and retiring in the evening. The manner in which social contacts are made and maintained will change, as will professional and recreational interests. Among other adjustments will be the change in sexual patterns. Obviously it would be a great mistake to attempt to bring long-established traditions of a previous relationship into a subsequent marriage. Particularly in this realm, sensitivity to the uniqueness of each person is most critical. With proper consideration for the spouse's distinctiveness, both partners can find themselves richly fulfilled in the bonds created by marital love.

Since the second marriage of Abraham is reported two chapters after the death of Sarah, it naturally would be assumed that Abraham married Keturah after the death of Sarah. Yet this assumption cannot actually be proven. Often it is overlooked that Scripture indicates that Abraham had a multiple of concubines (Gen. 25:6), and Keturah may have been among these partners of the patriarch.[24] On the other hand, it may be noted that with the marriage of Isaac after the death of Sarah, Abraham was left altogether alone in his home. As a consequence, he would have had strong motivation for entering into a second marriage.

In any case, under certain circumstances a second marriage may be legitimate, in every way proper, appropriate, and blessed of God. In the event of the death of a spouse, or if a marriage partner has been guilty of adultery or willful desertion, a second marriage may be the good will of God for a person (Rom. 7:2–3; Matt. 19:9; 1 Cor. 7:15). Such a second marriage is in no way required, but it could be part of God's plan for a person's life. As such, a second marriage may be wondrously blessed of him.

THREE

SEX AND SUCCEEDING GENERATIONS

■ ■ ■ ■ ■

THE COVENANTAL OFFSPRING
BARRENNESS
THE SINGLE PARENT
THE THIRD GENERATION

THE COVENANTAL OFFSPRING

I will establish my covenant as an everlasting covenant between
me and you and your descendants after you for the generations to
come, to be your God and the God of your descendants after you.
—*Genesis 17:7*

One of the most glorious aspects of God's creational activity was the establishment of the family. This same glorious intention for the family may be found in God's purposes in redemption. Despite the disruptions of the God-intended order for humankind as they are manifested in the abuses of human sexuality through bigamy, adultery, homosexuality, and divorce, God in redemption has reestablished the solidarity of the family through the institution of his covenant. This fact becomes evident with the first usage of the term "covenant" in the Bible, and continues throughout the progressive unfolding of the divine covenant as revealed in Scripture.

Because of the increase of wickedness among humanity, the Lord determined that he would bring floodwaters on the earth as a purifying judgment (Gen. 6:17). But with Noah God makes a promise:

> But I will establish my covenant with you, and you will enter the ark—you and your sons and your wife and your sons' wives with you. (Gen. 6:18)

With this first use of the term "covenant" in Scripture, God makes it plain that he will deal covenantally with families and not merely with individuals. His commitment is to restore the blessedness of the family unit that had been violated by humankind's fall into sin. It is not only Noah that shall be saved from the well-deserved judgment of the flood. His sons, his wife, and his sons' wives with him shall enter the ark of salvation. God's solemn covenant seals the certainty of this deliverance for the family of Noah.

This intention of the Lord to deal covenantally with families was reinforced at the critical moment when the time arrived for entry into the ark. For the Lord then said to Noah:

> Go into the ark, you and your whole family, because I have found *you* righteous in this generation. (Gen. 7:1)

The ambiguity of the pronoun "you" in contemporary English obscures the clear intent of the original text of Scripture. The "you" of this verse is singular, not plural. Its intent is to indicate that the whole family of Noah is to be saved from the outpouring of God's wrath because Noah as the head of this family unit has been found righteous. It is not that Noah's faith substitutes for faith on the part of the other members of his family. But since Noah has found grace in the eyes of the Lord, his whole house will benefit from God's blessing.

This same principle is continued in each and every one of God's successive covenants as they are manifested across the ages. Abraham is told that God will establish an everlasting covenant with him and his seed after him for the generations to come (Gen. 17:7). This covenantal bond with the patriarch and his family is not to be re-garded merely as promising certain earthly, temporal blessings. In-stead, the commitment across the generations is that this God will be the God of Abraham and his descendants after him (Gen. 17:8).

In similar fashion, the covenantal document of Deuteronomy begins and ends with clear reference to the fact that the divine commitment in the covenant reaches across the generations. At Sinai (Horeb), God made his covenant not merely with the gener-ation that subsequently fell in the wilderness. Instead, those chil-dren yet to be born during the forty years of wandering also were included in the covenantal bond at Sinai, even though they had not yet come into existence (Deut. 5:2–3). In sealing this newborn generation in a bond with God at the time of the renewal of the covenant in the plains of Moab, Moses indicates that the whole community has been assembled for this solemn occasion, includ-ing "your leaders and chief men, your elders and officials, and all the other men of Israel, together with your children and your wives, and the aliens living in your camps" (Deut. 29:10–11). No one from the community is missing from this covenant-renewal as-sembly. Yet Moses declares:

> I am making this covenant, with its oath, not only with you who are standing here with us today in the presence of the LORD our God but also with those who are not here today. (Deut. 29:14–15)

But who was missing from the covenant assembly? Who was not present? By the reference to people not then present at the covenanting assembly, Moses includes unborn future generations in the bond of the covenant. Family members yet to be born belong to the community of the covenant.

Both Scripture and experience indicate that this covenantal bond with the family does not automatically guarantee the salvation of each individual in a family. Disbelieving members will be cut off from the blessings of the covenant they have broken. Yet the intent of the covenant to include family members is quite evident.

In this regard, a special word may be addressed to those who have had the privilege of growing up as children of the covenant: "Don't break the chain!" If you depart from the privileges associated with covenant life, the effect may be that the blessings of the covenant will be denied to the third and fourth generation of those that follow you in your family (Exod. 20:5).

In a way similar to the flowing of blessings across the generations in the covenants with Noah, Abraham, and Moses, God's covenant with David also stretches across the generations to include his sons. Because of the divine commitment in the covenant, his house and kingdom will endure forever (2 Sam. 7:16). Once again, following the pattern found in previous covenantal administrations, God binds himself to the "house" of Judah and the "house" of Israel in the gracious provisions of the new covenant (Jer. 31:31). So it should not be surprising to find regular indicators that children and households are bound in this consummative covenant of God's grace (Acts 2:39; 10:2; 16:14–15, 31–33; 1 Cor. 1:16).

This bond of the covenant with the family unit of the believer should be a significant factor in every Christian marriage. One of the greatest manifestations of God's grace is the working of redemption for entire family units, and not merely for individuals. It would be a sad situation indeed if married believers who are in the covenant with God could only expect alienation from their children, who would remain outside the covenant. For a house divided against itself cannot stand (Matt. 12:25).

Often married couples of the current generation honestly ask the question, "Why should we have children?" If there are already enough children in the world, why should either partner in the marriage interrupt career advancement to add one more child to the mass of humanity?

Birth control may be affirmed as an appropriate method of relieving the woman from her curse of pain in childbirth that came as a consequence of the original sin. Just as man does what he can to relieve himself of laboring "by the sweat of [his] brow," so womankind may be relieved of excessive pains and sorrows in the bearing of children. At the same time, the restraints placed on the number of children being born must be balanced by the responsibility to fulfil the creational ordinance requiring that mankind be fruitful and multiply. Couples should rejoice in the privilege of bearing children just because their Creator has ordained this method for the multiplication of creatures uniquely made in his likeness and image.

The promise of God's redemptive covenant that embraces the generations to come provides an additional response to the question why people should have children. Christian couples should have children despite all the inconvenience and bother they might bring because an integral aspect of God's redemptive covenant is

directed to the divine promise that stretches across the generations. God's plan for the ages includes the peculiar blessings that
come only through experiencing the joys of seeing his grace extended to children's children.

■ ■ ■ ■ ■

BARRENNESS

Now Sarai [Sarah] was barren; she had no children.
—Genesis 11:30

The book of Genesis in a very distinctive way may be designated as the book of generations. Already it has been noted that
ten times over the phrase "these are the generations of . . ." occurs
in this first book of the Bible. Chapters 10 and 11 of Genesis are
taken up largely with the matter of the generations of humankind.
First, in chapter 10 a record is given of all the various communities
of peoples that repopulated the earth as the descendants of Noah's
sons after the flood. Then chapter 11 traces the line of Shem down
to Abraham as the one chosen of God to serve as the single individual through whom the blessing of salvation would be transmitted to the whole of humanity. It would appear that the order of
these two genealogies intends first to display God's interest in the
totality of humankind (Gen. 10) before tracing the designated line
through which salvation would come (Gen. 11).

Given this context, the interjection of the statement concerning
Abraham's wife at the end of the second genealogy is striking: "Now

Sarai was barren; she had no children" (Gen. 11:30). After two chapters devoted to genealogy, the climax is reached with a barren woman!

Abraham and his wife Sarah experience great strain in their marriage because of her barrenness. God had promised that through Abraham all the nations of the earth would be blessed. Yet Sarah has no children through whom the blessing may be transmitted. Abraham's descendants are to be as numerous as the stars of heaven. Yet Sarah slips into her declining years without once conceiving. The seed of Abraham is to possess all the land of Canaan. Yet Sarah is incapable of presenting him with a single heir. This whole experience of prolonged barrenness was a tremendous test to the faith of both Abraham and Sarah.

Now it is ten years after God's first promise to the patriarch. Month after month for over one hundred months the couple had looked eagerly for a sign that she had conceived. Yet Sarah's barrenness continues just as it had been described when she was first mentioned in Genesis (Gen. 16:1; cf. Gen. 11:30). Sarah shows her full awareness of the Lord's role in this perplexing situation. "The LORD has kept me from having children," she says (Gen. 16:2). She understands that her circumstance, as disappointing as it may be, arises out of the sovereign appointments of the Lord.

If the narrative had stopped at that point, it would have been a great testimony to Sarah's faith. By her own confession, she acknowledges that it is the Lord who has kept her from bearing children. In this respect, Sarah's faith in God's sovereignty may serve as an example to be followed by people who have no children today, even though they greatly desire them. Whether a person remains unmarried and so has no children, or has no children after many years of marriage, the response of faith should be the same. The Sovereign Lord must be trusted as the all-wise, loving heavenly Father who always has the best interests of his children in view.

Yet in her desperation to provide an offspring for her husband, Sarah resorts to a common custom of the day. She proposes that Abraham take this matter into his own hands. Abraham should receive Hagar, Sarah's Egyptian maidservant, as his concubine so he can raise up children through her.

Abraham yields to the proposal of his wife. Although most often a man's wife may serve as his best and most reliable confidante, in this case Sarah serves as a tool of Satan, tempting Abraham to sin. The language of Scripture at this point closely parallels the description of the mistake of the original man in the garden. On the one hand, God said to Adam: "You have listened to the voice of your wife" (Gen. 3:17 NASB). On the other, the narrator of Genesis reports: "Abram listened to the voice of Sarai" (Gen. 16:2 NASB). In each case, the wife becomes the tool of the tempter, and the husband yields to her proposal.

The further involvement of Sarah in this development is seen in the explicit language of the narrative: "So . . . Sarai took . . . Hagar . . . to her husband" (Gen. 16:3). Contrary to the normal possessiveness of a spouse, Sarah initiates this extramarital relationship of her husband. The length of the trial has finally got the best of her.

Sarah's proposal works, at least insofar as Abraham's having an offspring is concerned. But almost instantly Sarah is disgusted with the situation that she herself has created.

Ancient Near Eastern parallels to the biblical narrative may help explain the actions of Abraham and Sarah.[1] In their own minds, they may have thought of themselves as simply conforming to the customary practices of the day. Yet this explanation does not excuse them for their deficiency in faith. In any case, the parallels to ancient texts underscore the universal character in time and space of the problem of barrenness.

The proper solution to Sarah's barrenness is ultimately provided by the Lord himself. As a result of God's own miraculous intervention, Sarah herself shall conceive and bear a son. All through this time of testing, God has been establishing that the saving seed for humanity must be provided supernaturally. In response to this announcement from the angelic messengers, Sarah cannot contain her incredulity and laughs within herself (Gen. 18:12). The Lord who knows all detects the skeptical nature of her response, and affirms his unlimited power as God to bring about things impossible for men. "Is anything too hard for the LORD?" he asks (Gen. 18:14).

The barrenness of Sarah was indeed a special case. Yet a number of other women who were appointed by God to stand in the line that eventually would lead to the coming Savior of men had similar experiences. Both Rebekah the wife of Isaac and Rachel the wife of Jacob wrestled much of their lives with the burden of barrenness (Gen. 25:21; 29:31; 30:22). Through the experiences of these barren women, God was driving home the point that the saving seed would have to be supernaturally provided.[2] Only divine intervention could produce a Savior for humankind.

Many Christian couples today must face the difficult problem of barrenness. A sense of missing God's blessing by not having children can cause great distress. But husbands and wives must give themselves over to the good providence of God that determines all things for their good and his glory.

In the case of some, God may not see fit to provide a marriage partner to a person who wishes very much to be married and have children. Many single people have difficulty accepting their circumstance.

The proper reaction to unwanted barrenness will arise out of an unwavering faith in the good purposes of the Lord. He never makes a mistake. As a loving heavenly Father, he dispenses his good will in ways and for reasons that are not always clear to his people. In the case of some, the adoption of children may be God's good intention for them. Particularly in Africa today, the AIDS epidemic has left literally millions of children without earthly parents. Aging, impoverished grandparents are being given responsibilities regarding the raising of their grandchildren that they are hardly capable of fulfilling. One possible solution may be a widespread adoption of orphans by Christian couples that have no children of their own.

In other cases, the "spiritual" adoption of young people by sponsoring adult Christians may provide a very meaningful solution to barrenness for many couples. Older Christian couples who have no children may be well equipped to offer prayers, counsel, and encouragement to young Christians who may not have the advantage of believing parents.

Of course, it must not be forgotten that the Almighty has the power to intervene whenever he will. The conception of a child uniquely comes as an appointment of the Lord, for whom nothing is too hard (Gen. 18:14; Luke 1:37). It would be well for people who are accustomed to controlling virtually everything in their lives to remember that only God can cause a woman to conceive a child. This fact alone should make people stand in awe of every conception that occurs. It should also give unending hope to those believers who must struggle many years with the burden of barrenness.

■ ■ ■ ■ ■

THE SINGLE PARENT

The angel of God called to Hagar from heaven and said to her,
"What is the matter, Hagar? Do not be afraid; God has heard
the boy crying as he lies there." —Genesis 21:17

Difficult enough is the task for two parents to raise a child. Because of the vast diversity in human personality and need, the united resources of both a father and a mother will be exhaustively deployed in the loving, disciplining, and directing of their offspring. The stages of infancy, childhood, and youth will each demand the combined wisdom of both parents.

But one of the most trying circumstances of a fallen humanity occurs when the full responsibility of raising a child falls on a single parent. The entire task of training, counseling, and providing for the child frequently falls on the shoulders of a father or a mother alone. The already overburdened individual is required to take on a double load.

This burden Hagar the mother of Ishmael had to undertake as a consequence of her being driven out of the household of Abraham and Sarah. Her plight is first dramatized as she flees while pregnant into the desert, trying to escape the abusive treatment of Sarah (Gen. 16:7–8). But in her time of distress the angel of the Lord appears. He consoles her with the message that her descendants will be too numerous to count, and directs her to return and submit to Sarah (Gen. 16:9–10). Her child is to be named Ishmael, which means "Heard of God," for the Lord himself has responded to her miserable plight (Gen. 16:11). Yet at the same time she is forewarned that things will not go easily for her son, for he will be like a wild donkey, living in hostility toward his brothers (Gen. 16:12). Ishmael will be a "wild one," which often proves to be the case with children who have only one parent.

This troublesome relationship with his closest kin manifested itself in Ishmael's undisciplined teenage years. For an already overprotective Sarah saw him mistreating his infant half-brother Isaac. The patriarch's home could not stand such tension. As a consequence, Hagar found herself thrust out of the household a second time and placed permanently in the role of the single parent. Abraham sent mother and child off on their own with a provision of food and water. But in the dry desert near Beersheba, the supply was soon spent. In this moment of distress, Hagar displays all the pain often experienced by the single parent. She has no housing for her family, she has no food or water, she has no husband as a companion to share the burden of responsibilities. In her desperation she weeps as she lays her sobbing child under a bush, fully expecting him to die.

Once more the single parent may take courage from the experience of Hagar. God speaks to her in this desperate situation, and shows her a well of water nearby. She and her son are revived, and strength is provided for them to continue their journey (Gen. 21:9–19). Hagar's genuine need is met, not by a spectacular miracle, but by a clear divine intervention.

God continues to show his grace to Hagar in her role as a single parent. Scripture explicitly states that the Lord was "with the boy" as he grew up (Gen. 21:20). He lived in the desert as an archer. Eventually Hagar provided a wife for him from Egypt, and he became the father of twelve sons, chiefs of tribes that grew into a great nation (Gen. 21:21; 25:12–18).

In the redemptive-historical setting of the old covenant, Ishmael is set over against Isaac the son of promise (cf. Gal. 4:21–31). But it must not be concluded that as a consequence the descendants of Ishmael have been excluded altogether from God's work of redemption. For it is faith and not the flesh that establishes a person as a child of God. Sons of Isaac have no hope apart from saving faith in Jesus Christ, and sons of Ishmael become full members of the household of faith if they believe. God's care for Ishmael is stated explicitly in the Genesis narrative, and it may be assumed that from among the tribes descending from Ishmael's twelve sons will be many who confess Jesus Christ as Lord (Gen. 16:10–11; 21:17, 20; Rev. 5:9; 7:9). From the experience of Hagar it may be learned that the life of the single parent is a very difficult one. But by the appointments of the God of all grace it is not without its redemptive blessings.

Tamar, the bearer of Judah's children, also had to make her

way as a single parent. Judah was not true to his word that his third son Shelah would become Tamar's husband. Shelah should have been the one to raise up children in the name of his older brothers, who had been Tamar's previous husbands and who had been struck dead for their wickedness (Gen. 38:6–11). So Tamar took the law into her own hands. After the death of Judah's wife, she disguised herself as a prostitute and conceived a child by Judah himself.

Although Judah acknowledged Tamar's offspring to be his own progeny, he never again took her to himself as his wife (Gen. 38:26). Perhaps Judah simply could not contemplate living with this woman who previously had been the wife of two of his sons. Perhaps the thought that she actually should have been the wife of his now-grown third son served as a barrier in Judah's mind. Possibly there might have been a law or custom of the day that forbade a father from marrying the wife of his son.3 John Calvin concludes that Judah was manifesting the true nature of his repentance by refusing to cohabitate with his daughter-in-law ever again. He further asserts that Judah's restraint in this regard confirms the fact

> that by nature men are imbued with a great horror of such a crime. For whence did it arise, that he abstained from intercourse with Tamar, unless he judged naturally, that it was infamous for a father-in-law to be connected with his daughter-in-law? Whoever attempts to destroy the distinction which nature dictates between what is base and what is honourable, engages, like the giants, in open war with God.4

Whatever may have been the reason for Judah's not taking Tamar to be his wife, it would appear that the practical consequence for Tamar was that she had to raise her offspring as a single parent. Doubling the burden—and the blessing—was the fact that at the time of delivery she gave birth to twins. She may have lived in Judah's household and had the help provided by Judah's servants. But because Judah himself would not claim her as his wife, Tamar had to live the life of a single parent.

Tamar's life must have been a full and busy one as she raised her twin sons. The end result of her role as a single parent clearly underscores positive rather than negative factors. Many generations later, a distinctive blessing is pronounced over Boaz as he marries Ruth the Moabitess:

> Through the offspring the LORD gives you by this young woman, may your family be like that of Perez, whom Tamar bore to Judah. (Ruth 4:12)

In the mind of the elders addressing Boaz, God's blessing on Tamar was equal to his blessing on Rachel and Leah (see Ruth 4:11).

Eventually the line of descendancy from Tamar leads through David and the kings of Judah to its climax in Jesus Christ the incarnate Son of God (Matt. 1:1, 3). Clearly, single parenthood, despite its multiplicity of problems, must not be regarded as a circumstance without redeeming features. Tamar's conception of her sons and her resulting task of single parenting may appear as one of the most bizarre situations that could be imagined. But if God's grace can bless despite the peculiarity of these circumstances, then the most unusual of current situations should not lead to despair. Instead, the single parent always may live in hope that the Lord himself will take up the role of the missing partner in raising offspring.

A further basis of hope for the single parent may be derived from the observation that even Mary the mother of Jesus possibly lived the bulk of her life as a single parent. It is true that Scripture talks about brothers to Jesus (Matt. 12:47). Joseph presumably would be included in the reference to Jesus' "parents" at his boyhood appearance in the temple (Luke 2:41–43). But the very fact that Joseph is never mentioned beyond this point supports the supposition that he may have been older than Mary, and may have died before the children reached maturity. Joseph was a godly man, devoted to the Lord. Yet it is Mary's heart that shall be pierced with sorrow (Luke 2:35). Only Mary is mentioned as being present at the wedding in Cana (John. 2:1–5), and Mary, but not Joseph, came to see Jesus after he had begun his teaching ministry (Luke 8:19). The special concern for his mother shown by Jesus as she stands at the foot of his cross suggests that she had no living husband to care for her (John 19:25). In addition, Mary along with Jesus' brothers is mentioned among the disciples that joined in prayer after Jesus' resurrection, although no word is said about Joseph (Acts 1:14).

The cumulative evidence of these references suggests that at some point Mary found herself in the role of the single parent. Her children may have been grown by that time, but as is generally recognized, the process of parenting never ends. Mary's deep sorrow in seeing her firstborn son rejected, abused, ridiculed, and crucified she had to bear without the support of a life-companion. Any contemporary single parent who experiences deep distress because of the many troubles that may befall a child can know that even the mother of our Lord has experienced such pain, and has triumphed by faith.

But single parenting does not consist only in pain. Mary also knew the exhilarating joys of the resurrection of her son. Even though she may not have had a spouse to share with her in these great moments, yet her delight must have been unbounded. For God had done an unbelievably great thing in the exaltation of her son. Though she could not in any way claim credit for the glories of the eternal Son of God, yet without question she was uniquely blessed by the Lord among women (Luke 1:42).

The lot of the single parent is not an easy one. But the God of all grace has his distinctive ways of compensation. For as the apostle Paul has said in another context, "when I am weak, then I am strong" (2 Cor. 12:10). The weakness felt by the single parent can become a source of strength as a consequence of faith in the Lord.

■ ■ ■ ■ ■

THE THIRD GENERATION

Joseph . . . lived a hundred and ten years and saw the third generation of Ephraim's children. —Genesis 50:22–23

"If I had known that grandchildren were so much fun, I would have had them first!" So goes the saying that summarizes the blessing of enjoying your children's children.

When God the Creator first instituted sex, he did so antici-pating an offspring. It should not be assumed that marriage exists only or even primarily for the purpose of having children. The wondrous genius of the Creator designed the union achieved in marriage so that it would satisfy the deepest need of the human person for communion, fellowship, and oneness with another per-son. But one of the amazing consequences of this union is, ac-cording to the appointments of a sovereign God, the bringing of children into the world.

But the fall! Has not man's fall into sin destroyed the expecta-tion of children? No, for the original command to "be fruitful and multiply" is deliberately repeated after God's judgment of the flood (Gen. 9:1; cf. Gen. 1:28). So having children is a part of God's re-demptive program. If a person is blessed with a long life, he may see this expectation realized in the children of his children. So he enjoys the blessings associated with the "third generation."

Look at the life of Jacob. He left his father and mother as a sin-gle person. He was seeking a wife. When he came back twenty years later, he had grown into a "troop." Still later, Jacob journeyed into Egypt. By that time his family had multiplied to seventy in number. Finally, while enjoying his old age in Egypt, he has the pleasure of pronouncing his benediction on Ephraim and Ma-nasseh, the sons of his son Joseph. God had blessed him with the experience of seeing his children's children.

But Joseph experienced even greater blessings in this matter of enjoying his children's children. Joseph reached the age of 110, and "saw the third generation of Ephraim's children" (Gen. 50:23). That is, he lived to see his great-great-grandsons.[5] The fact that he received these children on his knees indicates that even at this stage of his life Joseph still was mobile, sitting up rather than being bedridden.

So God blesses the marriage bond in a way that stretches across the generations. For eternity one of the endless joys of the redeemed will be a tracing backward and forward the saved of the Lord that belong to their genealogy. Sex exists by God's appoint- ment not merely for personal pleasure, but for the blessings that stretch across the generations and into eternity.

FOUR

SEX AND SIN

■ ■ ■ ■ ■

SEX AMONG THE FIRST-FALLEN
CARELESSNESS
LUST
ADULTERY
RAPE
INCEST
HOMOSEXUALITY

Sex among the First-Fallen

And Cain went out . . . and dwelt in the land . . . east of Eden.
And Cain knew his wife. —Genesis 4:16–17 (KJV)

The fall of man into sin instantly and inevitably affected his sexual life. It is sad to see the many ways in which sin has put its ugly mark on human sexuality. But God's word does not ignore the many problems created by sexual sins. This degenerating effect of sin on sex is seen quite clearly in the earliest chapters of Genesis.

Cain the First Murderer

Cain the first man born of human marriage also proves to be the first murderer (Gen. 4:8). In marriage humans will produce children after their own image and likeness (Gen. 5:3). Adam and Eve were sinners who had rebelled against God's law, and their son Cain possessed the same rebellious nature.

So Cain was a destroyer of life. But through marriage he also produced life (Gen. 4:17).

But where did Cain get his wife? This question often appears first on the lips of those who have an inherent skepticism about the Bible. But frequently these people misread the biblical text. The Bible does not say that Cain went and "found" a wife, implying that another group of humans existed alongside Adam, contradicting the creation narrative in Genesis. Instead, the text says Cain went and "knew" his wife, referring to the intimacy of the sexual relationship (Gen. 4:16–17). Elsewhere it is reported that Adam had many children (Gen. 5:4). So the simple answer to the perplexing question concerning Cain's wife is that Cain married his sister. Though this degree of consanguinity in marriage is forbidden later in the Bible because of the degenerating effects of sin, these principles were not in effect from the beginning.

Cain named the city that he built after his own son, which in this case provides a further indicator of the fallen state of men (Gen. 4:17). He does not consecrate his cultural advances to God, but to himself. This first child of human marriage attempts to build a dynasty that can be passed on as an inheritance for his son. But nepotism seldom works. It only brings disaster. One of the effects of the fall is that men, having lost possession of eternal life, try to immortalize themselves in their children. But children never are quite the same as their parents, and parents who aspire to have their children succeed them are usually blind to the most devastating faults of their offspring. They cannot see their deficiencies, and so they never correct them.

Lamech the Proud Bigamist

In his explanation of the Creator's purpose for marriage, Jesus indicated that from the beginning God intended that "the *two* shall be one flesh" (Mark 10:7–8*). But Lamech takes to himself two wives, and so contradicts God's order in creation (Gen. 4:19). Having murdered a mere lad, he boasts to his wives that he will avenge himself ten times more than God promised to avenge Cain the first murderer if anyone should attempt to bring him to account (Gen. 4:23–24).[1] In the heart of Lamech, retaliation rules the day—with a vengeance. His formula of seventy-seven vengeful acts in response to a single transgression is far more severe than the Mosaic *lex talionis* of one-for-one (Exod. 21:22–25). It may well be that in establishing the new covenant standard of response to offenses, Jesus deliberately echoes Lamech's ruthlessness by his dictum of mercy that his disciples must forgive an offender seventy-seven times (Matt. 18:22).

Despite the violation of God's most basic law about marriage, the sons of Lamech advance the cultural capacity of man considerably. One son raises cattle, another plays musical instruments, and a third works with tools of bronze and iron (Gen. 4:20–22). God manifests his common grace to all the fallen race through his treatment of this family. As Calvin notes:

> It is truly wonderful that this race, which had most deeply fallen from integrity, should have excelled the rest of the posterity of Adam in rare endowments. . . . Let us know then, that the sons of Cain, though deprived of the Spirit of regeneration, were yet endued with gifts of no despicable kind; just as the experience of all ages teaches us how widely the rays of divine light have shone on unbelieving nations, for the benefit of the present life; and we see at the present time, that the excellent gifts of the Spirit are diffused through the whole human race.[2]

Often the question is raised concerning the polygamous practices of the patriarchs. Abraham and Jacob both had several wives simultaneously. Yet no statement in Genesis specifically condemns this practice. May it therefore be assumed that at least during the patriarchal age there actually was nothing wrong with a man's having many wives?

It may be acknowledged that at these early stages of divine revelation to fallen man, the intentions of God for marriage are not made as specific as they appear at later times. Yet by the very way in which God created man and woman, the truth concerning marriage was communicated. Only one woman was formed from the rib of Adam, and only one woman was brought to him. Adam could not have had more than one wife without committing incest by marrying one of his own daughters. The very nature of the intimate union between husband and wife communicates the concept that "the two [and only two] will become one flesh" (Mark. 10:8). By slightly rephrasing the creational mandate, Jesus draws out the implications of the original statement of Genesis. "*They* will become one flesh" (Gen. 2:24) means "the *two* will become one flesh" (Mark. 10:8). By his modification of the wording, Jesus does not add a novel factor to the Genesis statement. Instead, he simply brings out an implied aspect of the text that was always present.

It should be remembered that the book of Genesis communicates its message in a form that is currently designated as "narrative theology." By this method, theological truth is embodied in a historical narrative rather than in generalized propositions. With this perspective in mind, it is not difficult to discover the point in the narrative concerning the multiple marriages of Abraham and Jacob. Abraham's wife Sarah cannot endure the presence of her rival Hagar. So she drives her from the household. The intense struggle between the two principal wives of Jacob continues until the day of

Rachel's death. After many years of married life, Leah explodes when Rachel proposes that Leah share her son's mandrakes: "Wasn't it enough that you took away my husband? Will you take my son's mandrakes too?" (Gen. 30:15). All this time Leah has harbored deep resentment against her husband's second wife. For Rachel's part, she cannot be content with the one son she has just now borne to Jacob. So she names him Joseph, meaning "May God add" to this one by giving me another son. She must triumph in her marital competition with her sister, and pays with her life as she gives birth to her second son Benjamin (Gen. 35:18).

In some cultures where polygamy is still practiced, it is often suggested that men do women a great favor by taking more than one wife. Otherwise, it is argued, many women would have to remain unmarried in a social context in which singleness works special hardships for women.

But virtually any investigation into the actual state of a polygamous situation will uncover the unending pains experienced by women in this circumstance. In one instance, a woman was the fourth wife of her husband, but she was his favorite wife. Somehow she fell out of favor with her husband. The woman's son reported that his mother became suicidal, and was saved from taking her own life only because of faith in Christ. In another case, a wife in a polygamous marriage on the island of Zanzibar explained that every evening she had to prepare a full meal for her husband, even though she did not know whether he would choose to come home to her that night, or to go to the house of one of his other wives. Her greatest source of satisfaction lay in the fact that she had a secret paramour of her own.

This kind of circumstance could hardly be regarded as a blessing to women. God has not so ordered it, and the narrative theology of Genesis clearly testifies against it.

Seth the Chosen Seed

Seth represents the hope of his mother Eve. When she names him "Seth," which means "to set," she appears to be giving expression to her early faith that a "seed" will come from the woman who will reverse the curse that she saw fulfilled in the murderous death of her second son (cf. Gen. 3:15). The designation of Seth as the one "set" to be her "seed" supports the idea that Eve was thinking in terms of the first promise of a Redeemer given at the time of the fall into sin. God has "set" this "seed" in the place of his fallen brother (Gen. 4:25). A similar hope for a child who would remove the curse finds more explicit expression by (a second) Lamech, who names his son Noah, which means "Rest." By this naming of his son, Lamech expresses his hope that this son will be the one to remove the curse from the ground as God had promised (Gen. 5:29; cf. Gen. 3:15–19).

■ ■ ■ ■ ■

CARELESSNESS

So Pharaoh . . . said, "Why didn't you tell me
she was your wife?" —Genesis 12:18

Because of a lack of appreciation for the significance of sex in the modern world, people often treat sexual relations rather carelessly. Young people sometimes assume that reaching the age of physical maturity justifies an exploratory attitude toward sex. Generally there is little or no awareness of the consequences of these sorts of relationships.

But a casual attitude toward sex is not restricted to the young and inexperienced. More mature people who ought to know better frequently think they can have an affair for a time and then return to normal life, so long as they are not caught.

But the testimony of the book of Genesis concerning a careless attitude toward sex should serve as an adequate warning against anything less than a reverent, healthy respect toward sexual relations. A sobering corrective in this regard may be found in the relations among Abraham, Sarah, and Abimelech (Gen. 20).

Already Abraham had gotten into deep trouble during his sojourn into Egypt over a very similar matter (Gen. 12:10–20). At that time, he felt threatened because of the alluring nature of Sarah's beauty. He assumed that someone who admired her might kill him in order to claim her. So he persuaded Sarah to tell everyone she met that she was his sister, which happened to be a half-truth. But a half-truth is a whole lie. As a consequence of his misrepresentation of the truth, the pharaoh of Egypt took Abraham at his word and brought Sarah into his palace.

But God who watches all the affairs of men is not so careless in his attitude toward sex. Abraham and Sarah were his chosen vessels by whom the saving seed was to be brought into the world. So to protect Sarah from being claimed sexually by the king, God sent serious diseases on Pharaoh and his household.

Somehow the king came to understand that these afflictions

arose because Sarah actually was the wife of Abraham, and that God was chastising him because of her presence in his house. The king's response was instant. He summoned Abraham into his presence, rebuked him sternly for his subterfuge, and had him ushered out of his country as an unwelcome guest.

It might be assumed that the pious patriarch would have learned his lesson. But when he journeyed with his abundance of cattle into the area of Gerar, he repeated exactly the same ruse with King Abimelech (Gen. 20). This time God shut up the wombs of all the women in Abimelech's household so that they could have no children. Then he revealed himself to Abimelech in a dream, informing him that he was living under a divine death-threat so long as Sarah was in his house. Abraham's lame excuse that Sarah really was his half-sister made little impression on the king.

How amazing is the folly of human beings in denigrating the sexual relationship. Before turning his wife over to the capricious will of a heathen king, Abraham had been told that his son would be born of Sarah within the year (Gen. 18:10). Was he now willing to risk Sarah's being impregnated by another man? Or if Sarah already were pregnant, was he willing to place the life of this child in jeopardy by turning her over to Abimelech?

The intimacies involved in the sexual relationship must not be treated with a flippant, nonchalant attitude. God in his wisdom and grace has created a most wonderful and mysterious way by which the life of a human being begins. This sanctioned relationship must not be treated carelessly, for the consequences are far too great. Only one man and one woman committed to one another for life should enter into this deeply interpersonal bond.

The apostle Paul repudiates a careless attitude toward the sexual relationship when he says:

> The body is not meant for sexual immorality, but for the Lord, and the Lord for the body. . . . Do you not know that your bodies are members of Christ himself? Shall I then take the members of Christ and unite them with a prostitute? Never! Do you not know that he who unites himself with a prostitute is one with her in body? (1 Cor. 6:13b–16a)

In his hollow sophistication, modern man has deprecated the significance of human bodily relationships. Regarding himself as little more than a different form of animal, man has assumed that his body may be joined sexually with any number of partners in various circumstances without harming himself or anyone else. But the complex character of man's psychosomatic nature means that joining sexually with another human being actually unites him with that person, body and soul. Paul drives home the significance of the human body by noting that the believer in Jesus Christ is united *in his body* with Christ. It is not merely the spirit of a believer that is made one with Jesus Christ by faith. His body as well is united with him. For this reason, performing a sexual act with the body cannot be treated in a casual, careless way. The Christ of God who is united with the believer's body must not be treated so lightly. If serious consequences affected both the nations of Egypt and Philistia simply because of the possibility of an illicit relationship with the matriarch of all believers, how much more awesome will be the judgment that falls on people today who treat lightly the Christ who is in them by faith! The loss of joy, peace, and contentment that so often accompanies extramarital affairs may be regarded as the first of the divine judgments on those who fail to honor the sacred bonds of marriage.

■ ■ ■ ■ ■

LUST

Reuben went in and slept with his father's concubine Bilhah, and Israel heard of it. —Genesis 35:22

Despite all the beauty associated with the relationship between men and women as created by God, fallen humanity twists that beauty so that it becomes something ugly by the lust of the heart. Lust may be defined as an inordinate, improperly ordered desire in the human soul. Lust is often difficult to distinguish from temptation. But the difference rests in the attitude of the heart. Jesus defines sexual lust in terms of an action of the will that lies behind the lustful look. For the person who looks with lust already has committed adultery in his heart:

> But I say to you, that everyone who looks on a woman *with the intent of* lusting for her already has committed adultery with her in his heart. (Matt. 5:28*)

In the analysis of Jesus, it is the will, the illicit intent in the heart even preceding the lustful look, that distinguishes temptation from sin. Observing the beauty of a woman is a natural thing for a man. But a willingness to look with the prospect of possessing outside the limits set by God's law crosses the line and enters the realm of lust.

Once the illicit desire within the heart has been formed, the overt act of fornication or adultery often follows. It is not without reason that the Scripture says, "Keep your heart with all diligence, for out of it proceed the issues of life" (Prov. 4:23*).

The sin of lust is often accompanied by many other transgressions of God's law. The sinful act of Reuben with his father's concubine sadly displays the complexity of circumstances that this sin brings with it (Gen. 35:22).

Jacob had just lost his beloved wife Rachel as she was giving birth to Benjamin, her second son (Gen. 35:19–20). He had grieved deeply over the loss, and the pain of separation lasted for the rest of his days (see later in Gen. 48:7). Continuing his route of return from Paddan-Aram, Jacob pitched his tent near Bethlehem as he returned to his father in Hebron.

While he was living in this region, Jacob's oldest son Reuben shows a fatal flaw of character. The whole incident displays the sinister nature of evil, and the way it works in the human heart. In a most dishonorable act of lust, Reuben takes Bilhah the concubine of his father, the servant-girl of the just deceased Rachel, and lies with her (Gen. 35:22). How long Reuben had harbored this lust in his heart cannot be known. But respect for order in the family never would have allowed the incident to occur so long as Rachel was alive. Bilhah was the first of the servant-girls given to Jacob (Gen. 30:3–4). Rachel had presented Bilhah to Jacob out of the frustration that had come from her own barrenness. Because of this connection, the two sons borne by Bilhah on Rachel's behalf represented direct rivals to Reuben's position of preeminence. As Rachel had said at the birth of Bilhah's son Naphtali, "I have had a great struggle with my sister [Reuben's mother Leah], and I have won" (Gen. 30:8). Reuben certainly would not have taken to himself the servant-girl of his own mother Leah. Instead, he shows his contempt for the rival side of the family by defiling Rachel's servant Bilhah.

Reuben's father Jacob/Israel heard of it. Because sexual actions by their very nature are private affairs that most often involve only two persons, it is easily assumed that no one will know about these matters. But somehow the most private of deeds quickly becomes public knowledge. Anyone who feels himself drawn to an illicit sexual relationship might consider thoughtfully the likelihood that whatever he does will eventually be spread abroad as common knowledge. A wise elder once said that if you want the world to know a certain piece of information, lead your closest friend into a field, stoop down, swear him to secrecy, and whisper in his ear. Then you can assume the world will know your secret by the next day.

Jacob's consternation must have been great. Since his beloved wife Rachel was now dead, it could be assumed that Jacob would treat Rachel's handmaid Bilhah as his consort. But now she has been defiled by Leah's oldest son, the firstborn of all his children. The heir apparent with the rights of the firstborn has disgraced the family name as well as himself.

The Scripture mentions no punishment of Reuben by Jacob.

But he reacts rather strongly at a later point in his life. Reuben's shameful act comes up subsequently in two different contexts, and in both instances his future standing in the family is drastically affected by this one act of lust.

First of all, when Jacob in old age was in Egypt, Joseph son of Rachel brought his two sons Ephraim and Manasseh before him. At that point, Jacob takes a decisive legal action which significantly determines the course of the future for the nation that will develop from his offspring. He adopts these two grandsons, Joseph's sons Ephraim and Manasseh, to be his own sons. Just as Reuben and Simeon had been his firstborn children, so Ephraim and Manasseh must now be recognized as his firstborn (Gen. 48:5). Since these two sons were Joseph's firstborn, by adoption they now have become Jacob's firstborn. By this action, Jacob has indicated his determination to set the descendants of Joseph over Reuben and Simeon.

This reordering of the position of firstborn in the family is confirmed in later Scripture. In tracing the genealogies of the tribes of Israel, the Chronicler notes specifically that Reuben was removed from his favored position as firstborn because of his lustful act of incest, and was replaced by Ephraim and Manasseh:

> The sons of Reuben the firstborn of Israel (he was the firstborn, but when he defiled his father's marriage bed, his rights as firstborn were given to the sons of Joseph son of Israel; so he could not be listed in the genealogical records in accordance with his birthright, and though Judah was the strongest of his brothers and a ruler came

from him, the rights of the firstborn belonged to Joseph).
(1 Chron. 5:1–2)

A fallen race finds it difficult to learn this lesson. But the reality remains. The price for succumbing to a lustful desire can be massive. In this case, the right of the firstborn in Israel was taken from Reuben because of his sin and given to the sons of Joseph. By lying with Bilhah the maidservant of Rachel, Reuben intended to humiliate the rival line of descendency from Jacob. But in the end it was Reuben and his descendency that were humiliated. Eventually Rachel's line receives the prominence, even to the point of the development of the expectation of a "Messiah ben Ephraim" alongside the anticipation of a "Messiah ben Judah." But there is no tradition of a "Messiah ben Reuben." For as the writer of Chronicles says, Judah was the strongest, and a ruler came from him; but the rights of the firstborn belonged to Joseph. This same expectation is developed in one of the significant messianic psalms.[3] According to Psalm 80, it is from the Joseph tribe that the "son of man," the "man at [God's] right hand" (a deliberate play on the name Benjamin), shall arise to deliver the Israel of God.

Still further sad reflection on the downfall of Reuben as a consequence of his lustful action appears at the time of Jacob's prophetic pronouncement concerning the future expectation for his sons. On his deathbed he recalls the years-earlier defilement of his bed:

Reuben, you are my firstborn,
    my might, the first sign of my strength,
    excelling in honor, excelling in power.

Turbulent as the waters, you will no longer excel,

    for you went up onto your father's bed,

    onto my couch and defiled it. (Gen. 49:3–4)[4]

The scepter will never depart from Judah (Gen. 49:10). Joseph will be a fruitful vine, with the blessings of the heavens above (Gen. 49:22, 25). But no prophetic word of prominence is spoken over Reuben even though he was Jacob's firstborn. Instead, he is marked by his own father as a turbulent man, as easily aroused as are waters, as a person who will never excel. Because he went up onto his father's bed in his lustful action with Bilhah, the blessing of the firstborn is taken from him forever.

The act of lust by Reuben cost him dearly. First, it set his character as a personality who was turbulent as water. This destabilizing action determined the course of his life. Secondly, his action of lust gave Reuben a reputation he never could escape. This one act, presumably done in secret, became the hallmark of his life. Thirdly, as a consequence of not being able to control his own passions, but yielding to the temptation of the moment, Reuben was destined never to excel. The subsequent history of Israel confirms this point. No prophet, no priest, no judge, no king is ever recorded as having arisen from the tribe of Reuben. A person who cannot control himself can hardly be expected to control others. Although Moses later names Reuben first in his prophetic pronouncements concerning the tribes of Israel, he can only give expression to a hope that his tribe will live on rather than die out (Deut. 33:6). In the triumphant Song of Deborah, Reuben is mentioned only by way of query as to why he stayed among the flocks at a time of national crisis (Judg. 5:15–16). This firstborn of Jacob's sons has lost his manliness.

A sensitive but vivid portrayal of the destructive powers of lust serves as the theme of Alan Paton's *Too Late the Phalarope*. Proving unfaithful to his marriage vows while simultaneously violating the taboos of his society, the leading character effectively destroys himself and his family.

Other instances of the destructive power of sexual lust may be seen in David's downfall as a consequence of his action with Bathsheba (2 Sam. 11), and in the shattering of the life of David's son Amnon as a consequence of his lust for his half-sister Tamar (2 Sam. 13). According to Nathan the prophet, David is "the man," the guilty one who has stolen another man's wife. As a consequence, he shall never have peace in his house again. David's son Amnon follows in his father's footsteps. He makes himself sick through his lust for his half-sister Tamar. In the end he lures her into his bedroom under a pretense of illness and then forces her. The telling comment of Scripture exposes the final fruit of lust. Immediately after the deed has been done, "Amnon hated her with intense hatred. In fact, he hated her more than he had loved her" (2 Sam. 13:15). The cultivation of lust produces a bitter fruit. The consequence of treating someone merely as an object of sexual desire degrades the person while destroying the bond between partners as intended by the Creator.

Sexual lust has massive impact in the lives of people. The grace of God is needed constantly to save a man from destroying his own life as well as the lives of others. In a new covenant context, the ultimate consequence of inordinate acts of lust is spelled out explicitly. In dealing with the corrupt situation of the Corinthian church, Paul indicates the eternal significance of sexual lust:

> Do you not know that the wicked will not inherit the kingdom of God? Do not be deceived: Neither the sexually immoral nor idolaters nor adulterers nor male prostitutes nor homosexual offenders . . . will inherit the kingdom of God. (1 Cor. 6:9–10)

Let those who are tempted beware. Let them flee like Joseph from every temptation before they bring themselves down once and for all (cf. Gen. 39:12). Let them flee youthful lusts which war against the soul (2 Tim. 2:22; 1 Peter 2:11).

■ ■ ■ ■ ■

ADULTERY

His master's wife took notice of Joseph and said,
"Come to bed with me!" —Genesis 39:7

Joseph had been sold into slavery by his jealous brothers. He then became a household servant to Potiphar, one of Pharaoh's officials who served as captain of the guard (Gen. 39:1). Because the Lord was with him even in these adverse circumstances, everything that Joseph touched ended up prospering. Potiphar could hardly fail to notice, so he set Joseph over his entire household. The only personal matter with which Potiphar concerned himself was "the food he ate" (Gen. 39:6).

But Potiphar's wife has a different concern. She notices this handsome, well-built young man who spends so much time in her house. She is attracted to him. Perhaps she is getting older, and feels the need to prove to herself that she still can allure a man. So she adopts the role of the "hunting harlot." She will entice this young man by offering herself to him.

"Come lie in bed with me," she says. No doubt the wealthy wife of Potiphar presented herself to Joseph in a most enticing manner.

But Joseph refuses. He reasons absolutely correctly, though certainly in a way that was altogether unexpected by Potiphar's wife. His master, her husband, has entrusted him with the whole of his household. How could he possibly violate this trust? How could he sin *against* God (Gen. 39:9)? Obviously Joseph would be breaking the trust of his master if he accepted the proposal of Potiphar's wife. But his strength in refusing her tempting offer rests on more solid ground. He would be sinning against his God, the one who was the ultimate source of all these favors.

Two elements in the resistance technique of Joseph are worthy of note. First, Joseph regards this woman as being another man's private possession—not in the sense that she is nothing more than a piece of property to her husband, but in the sense that she is especially treasured in his eyes. How could Joseph betray his master by stealing his wife, claiming for himself a treasure that clearly is not his? The attitude of the woman could not nullify the objective reality of the situation. Joseph could not violate the trust of his master.

The principle enunciated by Joseph would apply to an unmarried woman just as well. For it should be assumed that one day any particular woman may become the exclusive treasure of one man. Shall someone else then denigrate this one who some day will become the most precious treasure of another person? Certainly not!

Secondly, Joseph braces himself against the woman's tempting offers by constantly reminding himself of his accountability to God. How could he sin against *God?* Not only in the life to come, but also in this life God judges the sinner. The person who transgresses divine law will not go unpunished. The consequence of David's yielding one time to his lust for Bathsheba should be viewed as a very real prospect for every transgressor of God's law. Because of his act of sleeping with another man's wife, God pronounced sentence: David's own wives would be defiled publicly (2 Sam. 12:11–12; cf. 2 Sam. 16:21–22). In addition, for raising his sword against Bathsheba's husband in an effort to conceal his sin, the sword of violence would never depart from his own household (2 Sam. 12:9–10). God's ways are loving, but also just.

People who feel they might be tempted to yield to improper sexual relations should forearm themselves by considering these factors. Adultery is like taking hot coals into your bosom. You cannot do it without being burned. You would be stealing another person's most treasured possession, and God will take vengeance. You would be breaking one of God's most basic laws, and he will bring justice.

In Joseph's case, the hunting harlot will not be put off very easily. Day after day, day after day she approaches the young man. She must have used every imaginable device to lure him into her bedroom. But Joseph has made his commitment to the Lord. He will not yield, no matter how persistent she may be. He determines to avoid her as much as possible (Gen. 39:10).

Finally, on a day when the house is empty of other servants, the woman seizes Joseph's cloak, insisting that he come to bed with her. But Joseph sheds his cloak and dashes from the house (Gen. 39:12).[5] By such an action, he has sealed his own fate. Potiphar's wife turns accuser, proving the old adage to be true: there is no anger like the anger of a slighted woman. She tells her husband that this young Hebrew has attempted to force her. Joseph is thrown into prison, where he remains for several years. The cost of resisting the allurements of this woman was great for Joseph, but in his integrity he had no other choice.

Among the few themes developed by extensive passages in the book of Proverbs is the warning concerning the seductive woman. For committing a single act of adultery is one of those things that can ruin a man for life. Particularly for those who are called to the gospel ministry, the hard fact remains true. One act of adultery, and your ministry can be finished. As the book of Proverbs says:

> For these commands are a lamp,
>   this teaching is a light,
> and the corrections of discipline
>   are the way to life,
> keeping you from the immoral woman,
>   from the smooth tongue of the wayward wife.
> Do not lust in your heart after her beauty

or let her captivate you with her eyes,

for the prostitute reduces you to a loaf of bread,

and the adulteress preys upon your very life.

Can a man scoop fire into his lap

without his clothes being burned?

Can a man walk on hot coals

without his feet being scorched?

So is he who sleeps with another man's wife;

no one who touches her will go unpunished.

(Prov. 6:23–29)

Both men and women may be found hunting for an illicit sexual affair. In the modern scene, bosses often pressure their female employees, threatening loss of job if they do not comply with their proposals. In return for sexual favors, vendors may offer their wares free of charge to meet the desperate need of a single mother. Sometimes a person is placed in a situation that is difficult to escape, as was the case with Joseph. What could he do? He was in no position to quit his job. He hardly could tell Potiphar that his wife was attempting to seduce him. He did the best he could under the circumstances, yet he suffered greatly. But even though he had to endure false accusation, defamation of character, and imprisonment for his integrity, in the end the Lord established him in a much higher position.

Many people find themselves in an unhappy marriage situation. They "fall in love" with someone else, and the feeling is mutual. Sometimes people commit the folly of placing themselves in perilous circumstances. A minister may let himself be alone at the church while counseling a woman. Or he may make the mistake of stepping across the threshold of a home where he will be alone with someone of the opposite sex. All these circumstances may lead to the sin of adultery.

The maintenance of personal integrity while living in a society whose moral standards are corrupted is most necessary for the people of God who are committed to a life of holiness. One fall in this area can terminate a person's service in the ministry of the gospel for life. The standard of Christian behavior requires not only personal restraint; it requires also resistance to advances that may come from without. As the apostle Paul says:

> The body is not meant for sexual immorality, but for the Lord, and the Lord for the body. By his power God raised the Lord from the dead, and he will raise us also. Do you not know that your bodies are members of Christ himself? Shall I then take the members of Christ and unite them with a prostitute? Never! Do you not know that he who unites himself with a prostitute is one with her in body? For it is said, "The two will become one flesh." But he who unites himself with the Lord is one with him in spirit.
>
> Flee from sexual immorality. All other sins a man commits are outside his body, but he who sins sexually sins against his own body. Do you not know that your body is a temple of the Holy Spirit, who is in you, whom you have received from God? You are not your own; you were bought at a price. Therefore honor God with your body. (1 Cor. 6:13b–20)

So what should a person do when he comes to realize that he has violated God's standard of holiness in the sexual realm? Very possibly like King David of old, he may have suppressed his feelings of guilt, consoling himself with the standard of morality that is quite acceptable in the secular world. But now suddenly he can avoid his sense of moral impurity no longer.

The best course of action when guilt is recognized is to follow David's example when he was confronted by Nathan the prophet for his adulterous act with Bathsheba the wife of Uriah:

"You are the man," says Nathan. You are the person guilty of violating God's laws of purity.

"I have sinned against the LORD," replies David. Instantly he acknowledges his wrongdoing without further rationalizations. He confesses his sin with heartfelt sorrow before the Lord.

"The LORD has taken away your sin," responds the prophet. It is removed forever. You are restored to full fellowship with your heavenly Father.

"Yet because of the shame you have brought on the name of the LORD, you will receive certain chastening judgments," continues the prophet. Disciplinary chastenings of the Lord are not incompatible with his full and free forgiveness (see 2 Sam. 12:7–14).

So in the grace of Jesus Christ, full and free pardon for sin is available to the repentant who come to him in faith, humbly confessing their wrongdoing. The burden of past guilt can be removed forever, and even the chastenings of the Lord can provide healing and health.

■ ■ ■ ■ ■

RAPE

When Shechem son of . . . the ruler of that area saw [Dinah],
he took her and violated her. —Genesis 34:2

In the judgment of two contemporary "evolutionary psychologists," rape should not be understood as an act of violence, but instead as "a natural, biological phenomenon that is a product of the human evolutionary heritage." As such, rape should be perceived as an example of an evolved "mating strategy" committed by men who are particularly desperate to plant their seed.[6] With these views being spread abroad, it is no wonder that violence in the realm of sex has become a matter of serious concern in the present day. Both inside and outside the marriage relationship women find themselves in situations in which they are violated in an intensely personal way. Date-rape has reached epidemic proportions. In the very circumstance in which a woman rightly expects herself to be treated most tenderly, she finds herself sometimes brutally abused.

The Canaanite prince of Shechem raped Dinah the daughter of Jacob. It may be that Dinah herself was not altogether without fault. She took the initiative in going out to visit with the "women of the land" (Gen. 34:1). "We can surmise that she also had some natural desires to be seen by the young men of the city as well," says one commentator.[7] The youth and inexperience of Dinah may have been a contributing factor to the incident. She was a younger sister to Joseph, who is only seventeen years of age three chapters later in Genesis 37. It is not absolutely necessary that these chapters be understood as having been arranged chronologically. But it is quite likely that Dinah was at the most fifteen years of age.[8]

There would have been nothing in itself that was wrong with Dinah's going out to meet some of the women of the village. But it must be remembered that the patriarchal families had received repeated warning about the danger of association with the idol-worshippers that inhabited the land before they arrived. In addition, nothing is reported of Dinah's resisting or struggling against the advances of the prince of Shechem. It could have been her naiveté that allowed her to be led by the handsome stranger into an illicit relationship.

But in any case, the aggressive action of Shechem the son of Hamor the Hivite is regarded by Jacob's family unquestionably as a case of rape. Whether by force or by his suave mode, Shechem violated the daughter of Jacob. The fact that Shechem's father appears at Jacob's doorstep with hat in hand indicates that Dinah's brothers were correct in their evaluation of the situation. Dinah their little sister had been raped and now was being held away from home by a burly foreigner. All during the polite negotiations that followed, this raw fact could not be forgotten. Whether willingly or by force, little Dinah was being detained by the heathen Canaanites.[9] She was being held captive after having been violated.

The humanness of the scene is underscored by the love language used to describe Shechem's reaction to Dinah. "His soul was drawn to Dinah," say the Scriptures (Gen. 34:3a*). "He loved the girl," and "he spoke to her heart" (Gen. 34:3b*), phrases that may suggest a tenderness in the sexual relations he had with her. The depth of his emotional involvement may be reflected in the fact that he instantly urged his father, the chief ruler of the area, to acquire Dinah for him as his wife (Gen. 34:4). In describing the situation to Jacob's family, Hamor the father of Shechem explains that his son "has the affection of his soul set on your daughter" (Gen. 34:8*). The language anticipates a circumstance in which a man in Israel might see a beautiful woman among the people they have conquered and have his affection set on her (Deut. 21:11). In this instance, the prince cannot restrain himself from speaking up. As has been observed, "Young Shechem whose happiness is at stake cannot remain silent."[10] He will pay any dowry, no matter how great (Gen. 34:11–12).

But neither physical attraction nor heartfelt love can by any means justify rape. The forcing of one person on another cannot be justified, even within the bonds of marriage. In this case, Shechem had "done a disgraceful thing" (Gen. 34:7). The term describing Shechem's action is "an ancient expression for the most serious kind of sexual evil."[11]

The consequences of rape are never very pretty. The emotional trauma for the person who has been abused is impossible to measure. The conception of an unwanted child creates unending problems, even though God can bring blessing out of the worst of circumstances.

But rape also regularly brings in its aftermath the ugly consequences of bloodshed and war. When he first hears of his daughter's defilement, Jacob does his best to keep things quiet. The abuse of a woman brings with it a certain amount of shame, even to the innocent party. But somehow the word got out to Jacob's sons, who returned from the fields as soon as they heard. These brothers of Dinah were "filled with grief and fury" (Gen. 34:7).

In their disturbed state of mind over the mistreatment of their sister, the brothers of Dinah determine on revenge. When Hamor and his son Shechem offer to pay any price so that Shechem can keep Dinah as his wife, the brothers resort to treachery. Only if all the men of this Canaanite community will agree to be circumcised will it be possible for intermarriage between the two groups to occur. Shechem's father presents his case at the city gate. The men of the village are persuaded that they will ultimately become possessors of all that belongs to Jacob's family through the process of intermarriage. So a mass circumcision is carried out.

While all the Canaanite men are in a state of debilitation, Simeon and Levi, two of the older sons of Jacob, move in to take their vengeance. Dinah is designated as a "daughter of Leah," which means that Simeon and Levi were full brothers to her (Gen. 34:1). To avenge the disgracing of their young sister, these brothers mercilessly slaughter all the men of the city and rescue their sister Dinah from the house of Shechem. Then all of Jacob's sons join in pillaging the city, taking for themselves women, children, and cattle.

Father Jacob understands the far-reaching consequences of this radical action of Simeon and Levi. They have made him a stench to the people living in the land, who are far more powerful than he. If the Canaanites decide to attack, all his household will be destroyed.

This act of vengeance has consequences that affect the distant future. When an aged Jacob pronounces his prophetic utterance over his sons, he distances himself from the violent act committed by Simeon and Levi:

> Simeon and Levi are brothers—
> > their swords are weapons of violence.
> Let me not enter their council,
> > let me not join their assembly,
> for they have killed men in their anger
> > and hamstrung oxen as they pleased.
> Cursed be their anger, so fierce,
> > and their fury, so cruel!
> I will scatter them in Jacob
> > and disperse them in Israel. (Gen. 49:5–7)

Even though they are his own sons who acted with the intent of maintaining the honor and dignity of their family name, Jacob pronounces a prophetic curse on Simeon and Levi. Their fierce anger has led to a slaughter of innocent people as well as the defaming of the covenant seal of circumcision. As a consequence, the descendants of these two sons will never have a specific territory in the land of promise. Instead, their descendants will be dispersed among the other tribes.

God's mercy is seen in that the descendants of Levi are appointed specific cities scattered throughout the other tribes (Num. 35:1–4; Lev. 25:32–34; Josh. 21:1–42). But the Simeonites are required permanently to live a dispersed life within the territory assigned to Judah (Josh. 19:1–9). Already before entering the land of promise, the fighting men of Simeon had shrunk dramatically from 59,300 at Sinai to 22,200 in the plains of Moab (Num. 1:23; cf. Num. 26:14).

When these brothers took vengeance into their own hands, they did not solve the problem of the rape committed against their sister. Instead, they made matters much worse by committing an even greater sin. As Calvin notes:

> Shechem, indeed, had acted wickedly and impiously; but it was far more atrocious and wicked that the sons of Jacob should murder a whole people, to avenge themselves of the private fault of one man.[12]

"Never take your own revenge, beloved, but leave room for the wrath of God, for it is written, 'VENGEANCE IS MINE, I WILL REPAY,' says the Lord" (Rom. 12:19 NASB). A retaliatory act of violence can never remove the wrong done by a previous act of violence. God must judge, and the powers of human government have been appointed by him to punish evildoers (Rom. 13:1). When they fail in their responsibility, the Lord himself will avenge the wrong that has been done.

Rape is one of those ugly realities that are part of this fallen world. Since God's people must live out their lives among unregenerate sinners, instances of rape will occur. This observation is not intended in any way to minimize the evil of rape, but only to note its inevitability given the conditions that prevail among a fallen humanity. Only the grace of God in Christ can provide adequate wisdom for a proper response to these kinds of tragic circumstances.

■ ■ ■ ■ ■

INCEST

Let's get our father to drink wine and then lie with him.
—Genesis 19:32

Incest may be defined as a sexual relationship between close relatives such as parent and child, or brother and sister. After the destruction of Sodom and Gomorrah, Lot's two daughters got their father drunk so he could function as the father of their children (Gen. 19:30–38). At this point Lot had no wife and his daughters had no husbands. All their spouses, or potential spouses, had been destroyed in God's judgment on the cities of the plain. But the Mosaic legislation forbidding that a father have sexual relations with his wife's daughter clearly shows God's attitude toward incest (Lev. 18:17). Possibly the daughters of Lot assumed that no man would be willing to marry them since they were the only survivors of a cursed community.[13] Some commentators have proposed that looking down on the smoking cataclysm below, the two women concluded they were the only living persons remaining in the world.[14] More likely the daughters of Lot concluded that no men were available to them from their particular community, which by local custom would be the social framework in which marriage would be possible.[15]

Some effort has been made to justify the action of Lot's daughters. Says one commentator:

The action of the daughters in the opinion of the Bible is to their credit. They do not act to satisfy sexual lust, but to fulfill their destiny as women and to preserve the family. . . . They sacrifice themselves for it and their action testifies to magnificent heroism.[16]

This view totally overlooks the fact that, as Jesus subsequently says with respect to another sexual aberration: "From the beginning it was not so" (Matt. 19:8 KJV). In the ordering of creation, God indicated that a person was to leave father and mother in order to cleave to spouse (Gen. 2:24). It is never legitimate for children to have sexual relations with their parents, or parents with their children.

The daughters of Lot may have been influenced greatly by the depraved moral condition of the cities of the plain. "Do not be deceived: 'Bad company corrupts good morals' " (1 Cor. 15:33 NASB). Eventually the Ammonites and the Moabites as descendants of Lot's incestuous acts with his two daughters became the perpetual enemies of God's people. As a consequence, they were denied entry into the assembly of the Lord to the tenth generation (Deut. 23:2–4).

The sin of incest, despite its repulsive nature to both God and man, continues into the modern scene. Nothing in terms of societal development has curbed the abuse of children by their parents. The perverseness of the human heart continues unabated despite the sophistications of the present day.

This error in the ways of humanity manifested itself in the early days of the Christian church. Paul the apostle explains the proper response to such perversion in his first letter to the church of Corinth. He describes their situation as one so depraved that it does not even occur among pagans (1 Cor. 5:1). In this case, a man sexually possesses his father's wife, most likely referring to a second wife of his father. The Christians in this newly formed society responded in the way that seemed most loving to them. They refused to condemn the offender, and instead they embraced him in their fellowship as an expression of their love. They may even have been a little proud of their tolerant response to the shameful situation.

No doubt the reaction of the apostle shocked the Corinthian Christians. He denounced their supposed act of charity. They have introduced the leaven of wickedness into their community. Unless something drastic is done, this leaven of immorality will spread through the whole church. So Paul exercises his full authority as an apostle despite his absence from the scene. On the occasion of their assembling together he in spirit stands with them. By the presence of the power of the Lord Jesus, he directs them to hand this offender over to Satan that the sinful nature may be destroyed so that his spirit might be saved on the day of the Lord (1 Cor. 5:4–5).

People living in the sin of incest can claim no place among the household of God. They must be put outside the fellowship of the church as the only hope of their being saved from the corruption of their sin. The free grace of God allows for the prospect of their final salvation, but only if their sin is repudiated.

The reaction of Paul may seem extreme, particularly from the perspective of the modern climate of society where tolerance has become the byword. But it should be noted that the apostle sees harsh treatment of the offender as the only hope left for his salvation. So long as he is coddled in the compassion of the community, he may never be led into repentance for his sin, and so his soul will be lost. But when a violation of God's established order is properly treated, hope exists for every person. You may have been the victim of incest, or you may bear the guilt of a participant in an incestuous relationship. But in either case, healing, help, and hope may be found in Jesus Christ.

■ ■ ■ ■ ■

HOMOSEXUALITY

All the men from every part of the city of Sodom—both young and old—surrounded the house. They called to Lot, "Where are the men who came to you tonight? Bring them out to us so that we can have sex with them." —Genesis 19:4–5

"Sodomy" as a term has lost its significance in the modern scene. But the reality of the depravity continues to corrupt the core of society today. Massive efforts have been made, particularly by the media, to make evil appear as good and good appear as evil. Yet sodomy continues to bring down the moral standards of society.

The word "sodomy" finds its origin in the Genesis account concerning the inhabitants of Sodom (Gen. 19:1–29). Abraham's nephew Lot chose this area for his residence because it was the most fertile valley in the region. But in contrast with the luxuriousness of the environment was the extent to which the heart of man had departed from the life standards intended by the Creator.

It is noteworthy that many of the garden spots of the world today are heavily populated by homosexuals.

According to the Genesis narrative, God sent messengers (angels) to determine the extent of depravity that prevailed in the cities of the Jordan plain. These messengers stopped along their way to inform Abraham of the Lord's coming judgment. Abraham boldly pled for the few righteous people that might be living among the wicked. In response to Abraham's intercession, the Lord promised that he would not destroy Sodom and Gomorrah if he should find as few as ten righteous people among the entire population (Gen. 18:32). When the messengers from God arrived at the city, none of its inhabitants showed the customary hospitality of inviting them to spend the night in their homes. So Lot, a stranger himself, insisted that they come to his house. But in the middle of the night a vast number of young and old men began to pound on Lot's front door. They demanded that he send out the strangers that they might "know" them (Gen. 19:5). In this case, the verb "to know" serves as a modest circumlocution for "to have sexual relations with," as it does in other places in Genesis (cf. Gen. 4:1, 17, 25).[17]

The boldness of this community of young and old men in their depravity becomes proverbial among subsequent generations. A thousand years later Isaiah describes the corruption of his own generation:

> The look on their faces testifies against them;
> > they parade their sin like Sodom;
> > they do not hide it. (Isa. 3:9)

In order to placate their demands, Lot offers his two unmarried (but engaged) daughters to the unruly mob.[18] Apparently Lot's guests "were for him more untouchable than his own daughters."[19] When the crowd responded with an effort to break down Lot's door, the angels inside struck with blindness everyone milling about outside. After Lot and his daughters had fled for their lives, the Lord's judgment consumed the cities and all their inhabitants.

A second reference to homosexuality in Genesis very likely is found in the narrative concerning Noah's curse of his son Ham. After the flood, Noah planted a vineyard and got himself drunk. Then Ham entered Noah's tent and "saw his father's nakedness" (Gen. 9:22). Elsewhere in the Pentateuch, the phrase "to see [someone's] nakedness" serves as a circumlocution for "to have sexual relations with" (Lev. 20:17; cf. Lev. 20:18–19). Very possibly Ham committed a homosexual act with his father, evoking his father's curse. The depravity of Ham's action would explain the severity of the curse. The fact that Ham's son Canaan was cursed rather than Ham himself shows the awful impact that a sexual sin can have on future generations. Eventually the Canaanites as descendants of Canaan, the cursed son of Ham, manifested such depravity that they were driven out of the land at the Lord's command. Yet the grace of God is seen in the fact that only one of Ham's sons manifested the same depravity as his father.[20]

References to "sodomy" and "sodomite" have virtually disappeared from current parlance. Indeed, it may be appropriate to exercise restraint in referring to "homosexuals." But the biblical picture is quite definite in depicting the unrepentant homosexual as standing under the wrath of God for his sin. Even as Sodom and Gomorrah were destroyed for the depth of their depravity, so will unrepentant homosexuals eventually be judged for their iniquity.

A confirmation of God's attitude toward homosexuality from a new covenant perspective is found in the apostle Paul's letter addressed to the Christians in Rome. Sometimes the question is asked, "Are all sins equally wicked in the sight of God?" Generally the answer given to this question is a not too carefully considered "Yes, all sins are equally wicked in God's impartial eyes." But the evil of sin may be aggravated by a number of factors. A sin done repeatedly after a previous expression of sorrow and repentance is more wicked than a sin into which a person stumbles for the first time. The stealing of church funds by a trusted leader would be far more wicked than if committed by a stranger to the things of the Lord.

In a similar way, the apostle Paul presents the sin of homosexuality as being among the greater evils that can be committed.[21] In describing the degeneracy of mankind, Paul mentions suppressing the truth (Rom. 1:18), failing to give God thanks (v. 21), and exchanging the glory of God for images (v. 23). Because of these sins, God gave mankind over to a deeper depravity:

> Even their women exchanged natural relations for unnatural ones. In the same way the men also abandoned natural relations with women and were inflamed with lust for one another. Men committed indecent acts with other men, and received in themselves the due penalty for their perversion. (Rom. 1:26–27)

In current society, a large number of people would be offended by the description of homosexuality provided by the Scriptures in these verses. Homosexuality is represented as being unnatural, as an inflamed lust, as an indecent act, as a perversion. Indeed, it is most appropriate to show love, care, and appreciation for the person of the homosexual. Yet it also must be recognized that homosexuality is a particularly evil sin that deserves, like other sins, the wrath and curse of God. The homosexual, like all other sinners, must be confronted with the hope-filled call to repentance for his sin, and to faith in the death of God's Son Jesus as the innocent one who suffered the just penalty due to sinners for their evil deeds. Modern-day society may bend over backwards in accommodating the homosexual. But no favor is being done to these persons if the ultimate consequence of their activity is not somehow made clear. Homosexuality must not be viewed as something "natural." It is simply not correct to say that a person should bear no sense of guilt for homosexual orientation in distinction from homosexual action.[22] For although the doing of wrong may carry more blame than simply contemplating an evil within the mind and heart, nevertheless a person ultimately will be judged by who he is as well as by what he does.

At the same time, "hope for the homosexual" is a message that must constantly be presented as an integral aspect of the good news brought into this world by the coming of Jesus Christ. The door remains open for all to come and find life eternal in him.

FIVE

SEX AND SINGLENESS

■ ■ ■ ■ ■

THE UNMARRIED
LONELINESS
THE WIDOWED

THE UNMARRIED

It is not good for the man to be alone. —Genesis 2:18

It is good for a man not to marry. —1 Corinthians 7:1

The original creational order concerning marriage is quite plain. "It is not good for the man to be alone. I will make a helper suitable for him" (Gen. 2:18). Yet all people, generally at more than one stage in their lives, find themselves in a single state. During a person's early adulthood, after divorce or the death of a spouse, people are alone. Wartime makes people alone, as do certain job assignments. By God's appointment some people spend the largest portion or even all of their lives in singleness.

The creation of man in the image of God must not be so linked with the relationship of man to woman that it is denied that a person in his singleness is still fully in the image of God. The more detailed creation account of Genesis 2 indicates that the man first existed without the woman. This narrative should be read as a true and factual account of the order followed by God in creation, and not as a mythological tale.[1] The man as first created apart from the woman was fully in the image of God, even though the Lord himself pronounced that it was "not good" that he be alone (Gen. 2:18). This lack in the man as originally created did not refer to any deficiency in his essence which made him something less than being fully in God's image. Instead it re-

ferred to an incompleteness with respect to his function as a social creature.

The possibility of a person's being perfectly in the will of God
apart from a marriage partner is displayed vividly in the life of Jesus
Christ. He radiated the glory of God as a human being with a fulness that none other could equal. In a similar but not identical
way, all those who have been redeemed by Jesus Christ shall reflect
the image of God most perfectly in the age to come, when they neither marry nor are given in marriage (Matt. 22:30).

In the narratives of Genesis, several of the major characters
spend a significant portion of their lives in a single state. Isaac was
forty years of age when he married Rebekah (Gen. 25:20). Perhaps
as a noble but failed effort to reflect the pattern of his respected father, Esau was also forty at the time of his marriage to two Canaanite women (Gen. 26:34).

So how is a person to act during his days of singleness? In the
moral structuring ordered by the Creator, sexual abstinence is a
necessary aspect of singleness. Although they may not like it, people can live without a sexual relationship. People cannot exist without breathing, eating, sleeping. But they can live without a sexual
relationship.

Both sex before the full commitments of marriage (fornication) and sex with another person's marriage partner (adultery)
are condemned in Scripture (Exod. 20:14; Matt. 19:18; 1 Cor.
6:18; 10:8; Gal. 5:19; 1 Thess. 4:3). The use of various techniques
designed to avoid conception or disease cannot cancel the moral
negatives associated with sexual relations of a person in the single
state. The intimacy of the bonding of sex requires a moral founda-

tion that has been defined by the Creator. God is holy, separated, set apart from all other beings, and not to be treated as a common object by humans. In a similar way, the bonding of the sexual relationship sets two people apart from all others. They have become "holy" to one another, separated, and must never be treated as common matter accessible to anyone else in the intimacies of sex.

The single state as ordered in the providence of God should not be regarded as a bad thing. Periods of self-containment, of self-discipline, of being responsible altogether for oneself can have the effect of building character and reliability in a person. These times of singleness, whether of short or long duration, can also lead to a deepening of the personal relationship to God. The single person can grow significantly in the important area of his entrustment of life into the hands of Christ his Redeemer and of God his loving heavenly Father. In addition, singleness can be a time in which personal friendships with people of both sexes can be cultivated.

Significant also is the fact recognized in Scripture that a single person can devote himself wholly to the service of the Lord in a unique way. Some people have the special gift from God to be single all their lives. The apostle Paul's "It is good for a man not to marry" (1 Cor. 7:1) must be affirmed equally alongside the Genesis statement that "It is not good for the man to be alone" (Gen. 2:18). As the apostle indicates, an unmarried man or woman may be concerned only about the Lord's affairs, and may commit himself or herself in a unique way to advancing the cause of Christ. But married people naturally (and properly as well) are concerned about their spouses, how they can please each other (1 Cor. 7:32–35). As a consequence, their concerns are divided. Single persons should regard their situation as a special gift of God, taking full advantage of the unique opportunity that is theirs to devote themselves wholly to serving the Lord. Their singleness in itself does not automatically make them more "holy," as is supposed by some in the case of monks and nuns. But it does provide them with a special opportunity to channel their energies specifically toward the Lord and his service.

At the same time, the basic design of the Creator from the beginning has been that singleness would be the exception rather than the rule. In his good purposes, God has designed the perfect spouse for each of his people that are to live in a married state. Each partner is formed in the womb for the other. The Lord's original declaration that he would make a helper "corresponding to the man" may be applied specifically to each case of marriage in the Lord. At the same time, periods of singleness whether a person is younger or older should not be dreaded. Instead, these periods should be understood as God's special, loving appointments.

A person who is single but contemplating marriage need not wait for a special revelation from God indicating the one he is to marry. In faith a choice may be made, trusting that God will bless the union. As one writer contemplating engagement and marriage indicated, his efforts to determine exactly what life would be like with his prospective spouse proved to be a futile effort. Finally he realized that a basic ingredient in the marriage commitment is faith in God's ordering of the future.[2]

In any case, a person who finds himself in a single state, whether for a longer or a shorter period of time, should accept in faith his singleness as ordered by his loving heavenly Father. Quite possibly, the condition of singleness will not last forever—although it could.

■ ■ ■ ■ ■

LONELINESS

After a long time Judah's wife . . . died. . . . When Judah saw
[the woman dressed as a prostitute], . . . he went over to her by
the roadside and said, "Come now, let me sleep with you."
—Genesis 38:12, 15–16

Loneliness can lead to sex. A lonely person is especially vulnerable in this area. Great temptations for both men and women come to the lonely, either to commit fornication or to hasten into a bad marriage.

Judah, ultimately designated as the son of Jacob through whom the messianic king is to come, marries a Canaanite woman (Gen. 38:1–2). To preserve the generational line through his children, Judah acquires for his eldest son a wife named Tamar (Gen. 38:6). When this son is struck dead by the Lord for his wickedness, Judah shows respect for the levirate law, which requires that a brother-in-law marry the childless widow of his deceased brother so that his brother's name might be retained. So Judah prevails on his second son to marry Tamar as a way of raising up an heir for his deceased brother (Gen. 38:8).3 But the second son, anticipating that he himself might be robbed of any meaningful inheritance, repeatedly spills his seed on the ground to avoid impregnating

Tamar.[4] For this action, God also strikes the second son dead (Gen. 38:8–10). At this point, Judah promises his third and last son to Tamar when he reaches marriageable age, without seriously intending to fulfil his commitment.

Then Judah's own wife dies.

In his loneliness, Judah, while on a business trip, propositions a prostitute situated beside the road. He does not recognize this woman to be Tamar his daughter-in-law, who had disguised herself. Possibly Tamar assumed the role of a cult prostitute, drawing on the Canaanite traditions that may have been a part of her own heritage.[5]

When Tamar's pregnancy becomes evident, Judah pronounces a sentence of death by burning for her sin (Gen. 38:24). At that point, Tamar produces Judah's personalized staff and signet ring to indicate the father of her child. "She is more righteous than I," exclaims Judah (Gen. 38:26).

Tamar may be commended for waiting until after Judah's wife had died to "take the law into her own hands" so that Judah would fulfil his obligation to see that she had a proper offspring. But it does not appear that she was totally without guilt any more than was Judah. At the same time, it may be deduced that the underlying motivation of Tamar was something more than merely wanting children. She had lived in Judah's household, having married his firstborn son. Both Abraham and Jacob had been promised through divine revelation that kings would descend from them (Gen. 17:16; 35:11). It may be assumed that Judah had shared this expectation with the wife of his firstborn son. Tamar's determination to have a son may well have arisen principally out of the developing messianic expectation among Abraham's descendants.[6]

So the offspring of this unorthodox union becomes the bearer of the chosen seed that leads to the Messiah (cf. Ruth 4:12, 18). Eventually Tamar is named among the wise women in Matthew's record of the genealogy that leads to Jesus Christ (Matt. 1:3).

Unquestionably, loneliness can lead to sex. A desperate search for companionship can end in a less-than-perfect relationship. Men and women who find themselves in a single state should take great care in sealing an intimate relationship with the opposite sex.

It would never be appropriate to presume on the grace of God. The blessing that developed from the Judah-Tamar affair will not necessarily be the result in every case. But neither should despair ever mark the life of the believer in Christ. At God's appointed time, in God's appointed way, a proper relationship will be established, if that is his perfect will for the life of his beloved sons and daughters.

Aloneness can be accepted as a time for special growth in relationship to the Lord and to other people as well. Aloneness can be extremely painful, creating an aching in the heart that never seems to go away. Even a busy schedule with many friends and family all about may not alleviate the pain. Yet a period of aloneness in a person's life should be recognized as an appointment of the Lord that is filled with his good intentions for his son or daughter. This circumstance should be seen as a unique opportunity for personal meditation, reflection, and evaluation of the direction of one's life.

■ ■ ■ ■ ■

THE WIDOWED

Sarah . . . died . . . and Abraham went to mourn
. . . and to weep over her. —Genesis 23:1–2

Contrary to the pattern of the majority of cases in society to-day, the book of Genesis reports more instances of men than of women who lose their spouses. Abraham, Isaac, and Jacob all go through the pain of outliving their beloved helpmates.

Few circumstances of the human life-pattern appear as pitiful as the man who has lost his wife of many years. For so long he has depended on this one person for his daily sustenance and encouragement. His wife has been his bridge for social contacts in neighborhood, family, church, and business. Now he suddenly discovers the meaning of being a single misfit in society, of being the one who is often left out of the party and who has no proper means for reciprocation when he is included. Widowed women seem more equipped to cope with their changed situation. But the pain of separation is no less great, and the problems created by a radically different financial circumstance are generally much larger for a woman.

Reactions to a state of widowhood can vary greatly. Abraham grieved deeply at the time of Sarah's death (Gen. 23:1–2). But apparently he married again, although he may have been married to Keturah at some earlier point in his life (Gen. 25:1–4). Nothing is said of Isaac's remarrying after the death of his beloved Rebekah, which suits the fact that not a word can be found in Scripture indicating that he ever was in a polygamous relationship. Jacob had the dual burden of burying both Rachel and Leah (Gen. 35:19–20;

49:31). In each of these cases, life went on for a number of decades for these widowed men. By the grace of God they persevered in faith and made themselves useful in the kingdom of God even though suffering from the loss of their spouses.

Other cases of widowhood in Genesis are presented with more negative consequences. In the loneliness of his widowhood, Judah succumbs to the allurements of a prostitute while he is on a business trip (Gen. 38:12–19). Abraham's relative Lot is persuaded by his two daughters to drink too much wine after losing his wife in conjunction with the conflagration that destroyed Sodom and Gomorrah. In his semiconscious state he becomes the father of sons by his own daughters (Gen. 19:30–38). The loneliness and need associated with widowhood can occasion a serious fall into sin.

The experience of being widowed has its various stages. Often the beloved spouse comes down with a prolonged, debilitating illness. How distressing to see your life-partner degenerating, stumbling, becoming progressively weaker. There is the rushing about from doctor to clinic, from this medicine to that treatment. But eventually the inevitable must be acknowledged. Then there is the actual hour of separation that must be experienced. Family and friends gather—and then they are gone. The full weight of the separation floods in, and a sense of emptiness pervades every room of a person's dwelling. Finally there is the creating of a routine designed to blot out the loneliness that intrudes into every aspect of life. Waking alone, eating alone, returning home alone—being alone becomes a major factor for the widowed.

But the believer in Christ is never alone. If a proper faith is exercised daily, the time of widowhood can be a period of growing closer to the Lord. Even the hour of separation and the attendant funeral services can be moments of triumph through faith in the resurrection. As the psalmist says, "Though my father and my mother forsake me, the LORD will receive me" (Ps. 27:10). For some the times of tears may last for many years. But even those times can be precious if it is accepted that knowing Christ is better than life.

The apostle Paul had some sage advice that he addressed to the widowed. Although his words are directed specifically to women, some of the basic principles may be applied to widowed men as well. Younger widows are to remarry, so that the enemy of the gospel will have no basis for slander (1 Tim. 5:14). A dependent widow should be supported by family (1 Tim. 5:4, 8, 16). When no supportive family exists, the church should make basic provisions (1 Tim. 5:9–10). These arrangements all have the effect of encircling the widowed with the comfort and strength of the believing community. As a consequence, they are not left alone to find a way through life in their new circumstance. At the same time, the community of believers experiences the blessing of having incorporated the widowed more fully into their fellowship.

Throughout Scripture, the widowed are presented as receiving the special care of the Lord. God expresses his particular concern that the widowed be protected from any injustice or unanswered need (Exod. 22:22; Deut. 10:18; 24:17, 19–21; 26:12–13; 27:19; Ps. 146:9). Often people tend to draw back from a person who has been recently widowed. Even friends who have been close for years may feel awkward about an ongoing friendship, since they have built their social connection by relating as couples.

Nothing could be worse for the widowed. Instead of withdrawing from them, include them! Make a special effort. Invite them for a meal. If they refuse your first invitation, invite them again (and again). Make them feel they can drop over to your house without a special invitation. Be conscious of their special dilemmas. If they need a new roof on their house, give them a hand. If their children are sick or need transport, offer to help. Let your children be their children. Be "profoundly available" to them even when it's inconvenient to you. In doing these things for the widowed, you will help bear their burdens, and so fulfil the law of Christ.

Two of the most beautiful love stories in the whole of the Bible focus on widows. Boaz marries the widow Ruth in order to preserve the family name of her previous husband (Ruth 4:10–13), and David marries the wise and beautiful widow Abigail after the Lord has given her release through the death of her sullen husband Nabal (1 Sam. 25:36–42). At the time of Jesus' presentation in the temple, it was the widow Anna who met the young child. She had been married for only seven years and now was eighty-four (Luke 2:36–37). It may be supposed that she had spent as much as sixty years as a widow. But now at this late stage of her widowhood she has the privilege of welcoming the Christ child, giving thanks to God for him, and testifying to all the believers of his role as the Redeemer (Luke 2:38).

In each of these instances, the Lord compensates the losses of the widowed in his own time and way. The person who today finds himself in the difficult circumstance of the widowed should take heart and keep trusting. Never conclude that life is over for you if you are widowed, whether you are young or old. In time the Lord will show his good purposes even in the loss of a most beloved spouse.

SIX

SEX AND THE END OF THIS LIFE

■ ■ ■ ■ ■

THE GRAVE IS NOT THE END

THE GRAVE IS NOT THE END

Altogether, Abraham lived a hundred and seventy-five years.
Then Abraham breathed his last and died at a good old age,
an old man and full of years. . . . His sons Isaac and Ishmael
buried him in the cave of Machpelah. . . . There Abraham was
buried with his wife Sarah. —Genesis 25:7–10

The family burial plot puts husband and wife together at the end of this life. The book of Genesis witnesses to this fact in the case of several of the patriarchs.

Abraham and Sarah were already married when they departed from Ur of the Chaldees (Gen. 11:31b). How long had they been married in Ur? Scripture does not say. But most likely they were not on their honeymoon when they left for Canaan. They settled for a time in Haran on the way to Canaan (Gen. 11:31c). How long were they in Haran? Scripture does not say. But when they finally left Haran, Abraham was seventy-five years of age (Gen. 12:4). If Abraham had married at forty years of age, he and Sarah already had been married thirty-five years when they left Haran for Canaan. Sarah was ten years his younger, and so must have been sixty-five years old when the couple left Haran (cf. Gen. 17:1 with 17:17). Since Sarah was 127 years of age at the time of her death, the couple were married for sixty-two years after leaving Haran. If we take into account the time they had been married before leaving Ur, the period they spent in Haran, and the time of travel to Canaan, they must have been living as a united couple for well over seventy years. How close they must have been to one another after all that time. For possibly as much as fifty years of their marriage, they had only one another, with no children to divert their attention from each other.

How deeply Abraham must have felt the loss of his wife. How touching is the scene of this ancient patriarch, bent over his dead wife, mourning and weeping for her (Gen. 23:1–2).

At the moment of Sarah's death the landless character of Abraham's existence through all these years must have struck him with fullest force. Together with Sarah he had endured for decades the tension of having no son despite God's specific promise that his descendants would be as numerous as the stars of the heavens. But now he alone had to deal with the stark reality that despite the Covenant Lord's repeated reassurance that he would possess the whole of the land, he owned none of it. Perhaps this very moment, the moment of Sarah's death, was the occasion that forced him to believe in "a better country—a heavenly one" (Heb. 11:16). Since he had no land, God must have a land for him.

Abraham had to do something with the body of his beloved wife. Yet after over sixty years of traversing the land of Canaan, he did not even possess a single piece of ground where he might lay Sarah's body to rest with some dignity.

The scene is quite touching. Neighbors gather around Abraham at the time of his mourning. As he rises from beside his dead wife, he begins to speak to his Hittite neighbors. But what can he say? He remains a stranger in a strange land. He can only plead for their understanding even as he seeks to maintain his own dignity in behalf of his family:

I am an alien and a stranger among you. Sell me some property for a burial site here so I can bury my dead. (Gen. 23:4)

Working through a courteous Middle Eastern bargaining
process, Abraham first refuses to receive the land as a "gift." It
would appear that the intent never was actually to offer the land
free of charge. Ephron intended only to open the bargaining
process. Abraham then attempts to purchase only a cave suitable
for his purposes. But Ephron insists that the field also be included
in the arrangement. It may be that as a consequence of this process
Abraham was being forced to assume certain societal obligations
that would fall on him as a landowner in the community. He was
also being led into paying what appears to be an exorbitant price
for this small piece of land.[1] But at any cost he would have an appropriate place for the burial of his beloved Sarah.

In any case, a family burial plot is obtained, and Sarah becomes
its first occupant. The locale is a significant one. Hebron (Mamre)
was one of the first sites in Canaan where Abraham worshipped
(Gen. 13:18). Situated on the highest ridge in the southern part of
Palestine, it commands a broad view that stretches across the Dead
Sea depression to the east, and reaches to the shores of the
Mediterranean to the west on a clear day. This very site was destined for repeated prominence in subsequent biblical history, serving as the place where David first became king, and then sadly as
the point from which David's son Absalom launched his rebellious
effort to usurp his father's throne (2 Sam. 2:1–4; 15:7–10).

Thirty-seven years after Sarah's death, Abraham himself died.
His sons Isaac and Ishmael assembled to bury him. They placed

him in the cave of Machpelah near Mamre, the same field that Abraham had bought from the Hittites. "There Abraham was buried with his wife Sarah" (Gen. 25:10). United through life, they were united once more in their death.

This hallowed site was the final resting place not only for Abraham and Sarah. Isaac and Rebekah were also buried side by side in the same locale (Gen. 35:27–29; 49:31). Jacob, while still in Egypt, insisted that he be transported to this very spot so he could be buried with Leah his wife (Gen. 49:29–32). Seventy days were spent in Egypt mourning Jacob's death, during which time a full forty days were spent embalming his body after the manner of the Egyptians. After the preparations had been completed, a full entourage of Egyptian officials accompanied Joseph and his brothers across the Sinai desert to the land of Canaan, where Jacob was buried in the same cave at Hebron that Abraham had bought as a burial place so many years earlier (Gen. 50:7–9, 12–14).

But why? Why did Jacob insist on being buried in the land of promise rather than in Egypt? Part of his motivation must have been a sentimental attachment to the family burial place of his ancestors. But it may have been that his determination was based on a hope rooted in the promises of God concerning the possession of the land given to the patriarchs. Never had they experienced personal fulfilment of the promise spoken to them by the faithful covenant God. So either their God would prove to be untrue to his promises, or the day would come in which they would experience the realization of the promises just as God had said. It would not be enough simply for their descendants to possess the land, for the word of the Lord had been quite specific that they themselves would experience the joy of possessing the promise. As a consequence, the seed of resurrection faith apparently developed early in the minds of the first patriarchs. As the writer to the Hebrews says:

> All these people were still living by faith when they died. They did not receive the things promised; they only saw them and welcomed them from a distance. And they admitted that they were aliens and strangers on earth. People who say such things show that they are looking for a country of their own. (Heb. 11:13–14)

The logic of faith is irresistible. God gave the patriarchs certain promises. These promises were not fulfilled during the lifetime of the patriarchs. This God cannot lie. Therefore God's promises to the patriarchs must be fulfilled some day in the future.

The reason for the delay in the fulfilment of the promises is explained in Hebrews 11:

> These were all commended for their faith, yet none of them received what had been promised. God had planned something better for us so that only together with us would they be made perfect. (Heb. 11:39–40)

God has planned all along that believers of the new covenant should be united with believers of the old covenant in the possession of the promises. Therefore the believers of the old covenant had to wait to fully possess redemption's promises until that day in the future when they could be joined by us.

Until that day, the union that occurs in marriage remains a mystery that can never be fully comprehended. Two people become one in a way that defies precise explanation. By the grace that comes through Jesus Christ, this union becomes richer and richer through the years.

But what happens at death? What happens in eternity to this deep union with its physical, mental, emotional, and spiritual dimensions that has been forged through many years of life together? This too is a great mystery.

Many people are deeply disturbed by the idea that there will be no marriage in heaven, even though they may (somewhat reluctantly) affirm Jesus' teaching on the matter. Some people feel they will be "cheated" in eternity if they are denied a unique ongoing relationship with the one person that has been closest to them throughout this life.

People understandably struggle with this issue of the ongoing relationship of husband and wife in the life to come. One of the great sustaining truths for a grieving spouse is the anticipation of reunion that will occur in some future day. This anticipation is beautifully expressed by a Christian wife whose husband died just one month after the celebration of their fiftieth wedding anniversary. In her Christmas letter to friends she writes:

> This Christmas is one of deep emotion for me: great sorrow and great joy! The sorrow is that Harold died on September 22nd after a short struggle with leukemia, and I miss him beyond measure. The joy is manifold: he is with our Lord and Savior Jesus Christ, whose birth

we are celebrating; he is free from illness; and I will see him again.

So what can be expected at that glorious moment when spouses committed to one another for life see each other again? If people at the resurrection will be like the angels who "neither marry, nor are given in marriage" (Matt. 22:30 KJV), how exactly will this relationship be defined in eternity?

The best answer that can be given to this heart-felt question has been penned under divine inspiration by the apostle Paul: "Eye has not seen, nor ear heard, . . . what God has prepared for them that love him" (1 Cor. 2:9*). The apostle John adds his own divinely inspired insight: "Beloved, now are we the sons of God, and it doth not yet appear what we shall be" (1 John 3:2 KJV). It is true that Paul proceeds to say that God has revealed these things to us by his Spirit (1 Cor. 2:10). Yet he himself speaks of the bodily transformation that will occur at the resurrection as a "mystery" (1 Cor. 15:51).

The life to come for the redeemed must be viewed as something of a mystery because it represents the climactic stage of the grand divine plan that stretches from eternity to eternity. Because of this climactic character of the future transformation, it should not be surprising that the full purpose of God has not been revealed to mankind in advance of that hour. Instead, the experience itself will communicate the wonder of the Lord's climactic work. Although details cannot be known to us, the hope is certain that whatever we might imagine will be surpassed by the reality that comes to be.

We can know that because of this grand divine plan, husband and wife who have lived together will enjoy the fellowship of one another throughout eternity. Even though people will not marry or be given in marriage in the life to come, there will be the eternal enjoyment of one another in a fuller, richer way. Though marriage as it is known in the present age will not be experienced in the age to come, yet a wondrous fellowship will be enjoyed among believers through the eternal ages of the future. In this experience, whether single or married, none will find any dissatisfaction whatsoever.

CONCLUSION

Sex is one of God's greatest gifts to the human race. Mankind regularly misuses this gift. But the wisdom and grace of God in Jesus Christ show the way to restoration in a fallen world.

The book of Genesis is most remarkable in the thoroughness of its treatment of this grand theme. Modern man, with all his supposed sophistications, would do well to follow the way of faithfulness to this ordinance of God as revealed in the Book of Beginnings. He could then anticipate experiencing the fulness of God's blessings both in this life and in that which is to come.

NOTES

INTRODUCTION

1 The rendering "These are the generatings of . . ." best conveys the thought of the phrase, though this translation may not be the most suitable for the English Bible. Different English translations have rendered the phrase variously: "These are the generations of . . ." (KJV, RSV); "This is the account of . . ." (NIV); "This is the history of the descendants of . . ." (NLB). The phrase, sometimes slightly modified, occurs in Gen. 2:4; 5:1; 6:9; 10:1; 11:10; 11:27; 25:19; 36:1; 36:9; 37:2.

2 *The New Shorter Oxford English Dictionary*, ed. Lesley Brown (Oxford: Clarendon, 1993), 2:2801.

CHAPTER 1. SEX AND
THE BEGINNINGS OF LIFE

1 Claus Westermann, *Genesis 1–11: A Commentary* (London: SPCK, 1984), 232. While Westermann places the Genesis narrative in the category of myth, his comment on the significance of woman in the text is accurate.

2 Benno Jacob, *The First Book of the Bible: Genesis* (New York: Ktav, 1974), 21.

3 "On marriage a man's priorities change. Beforehand his first obligations are to his parents; afterwards they are to his wife" (Gordon J. Wenham, *Genesis 1–15*, Word Biblical Commentary [Waco: Word, 1987]), 71.

4 As cited in David Atkinson, *The Message of Genesis 1–11* (Leicester: Inter-Varsity, 1990), 71.

5 Gerhard von Rad, *Genesis: A Commentary* (Philadelphia: Westminster, 1976), 85.

6 John Milton, *Paradise Lost*, book 8, lines 471–78, 488–89.

7 John Calvin, *Commentaries on the First Book of Moses Called Genesis* (Grand Rapids: Eerdmans, n.d.), 1:97.

8 Ibid., 97–98.

CHAPTER 2. SEX AND MARRIAGE

1 John Calvin, *Commentaries on the First Book of Moses Called Genesis* (Grand Rapids: Eerdmans, n.d.), 2:11.

2 G. Ch. Aalders, *Genesis*, Bible Student's Commentary (Grand Rapids: Zondervan, 1981), 2:70.

3 C. F. Keil and F. Delitzsch, *Biblical Commentary on the Old Testament* (Grand Rapids: Eerdmans, n.d.), 1:260–61.

4 C. S. Lewis, *The Screwtape Letters* (New York: Macmillan, 1969), 83.

5 Gordon J. Wenham, *Genesis 16–50*, Word Biblical Commentary (Waco: Word, 1994), 2:152.

6 Claus Westermann, *A Thousand Years and a Day: Our Time in the Old Testament* (Philadelphia: Fortress, 1962), 182–83.

7 Aalders, *Genesis*, 2:216.

8 Keil and Delitzsch, *Biblical Commentary*, 1:352.

9 See Aalders, *Genesis*, 2:118.

10 *Good News Bible: Today's English Version* (New York: American Bible Society, 1976).

11 This interpretation builds on the old King James Version of the Bible which states that "giants" were the offspring of these unions, which in turn goes back to the term used in the Septuagint to translate both *nephilim* and *giborim* in Gen. 6:4 (*gigantes*). But the term in Hebrew does not mean "giants." Literally the Hebrew word *nephilim* may mean "fallen ones" or "ones who fall upon" others, meaning men who were brutal or forceful. The usage of the term to designate the inhabitants of Canaan that had been observed by the spies sent by Moses suggests that the *nephilim* were larger than normal size. They are described literally as "men of measures" that made the spies view themselves as "grasshoppers" in comparison with these sons of Anak (Num. 13:32–33). Elsewhere the descendants of Anak who inhabited the land of Canaan are described as "great and tall" (Deut. 9:2; cf. Josh. 15:14; 21:11; see also Deut. 2:20–21; 3:11; Amos 2:9). Presumably their larger size would not have been significantly disproportionate to the

height of larger-than-average men of today. But none of these references suggest that the *nephilim* or the Anakim were the offspring of supernatural beings or creatures from another world.

Despite the fact that the Scriptures elsewhere give hardly an iota of space for mythological interpolations in the narrative of redemptive history, modern interpreters of various theological stripes have tended to opt for the mythological view of this passage. Claus Westermann, *Genesis 1–11: A Commentary* (London: SPCK, 1984), 372, summarizes the current consensus by stating, "This [mythological] explanation occurs so frequently now that one can speak of a broad agreement," and then cites nine different authors supporting the mythological view. E. A. Speiser, *Genesis: Introduction, Translation, and Notes* (Garden City, N.Y.: Doubleday, 1964), 44, translates "sons of God" as "divine beings," proposing that the main stress is on " 'immortals' as opposed to 'mortals' " (p. 45). He speaks of the "undisguised mythology of this isolated fragment" that is "not only atypical of the Bible as a whole but also puzzling and controversial in the extreme" (p. 45). The acknowledgment that this passage, interpreted mythologically, is atypical of the whole Bible is worthy of note. Bruce Vawter, *On Genesis: A New Reading* (Garden City, N.Y.: Doubleday, 1977), 110, views the passage in a similar fashion. He says: "The original sense of the myth is not difficult to determine. . . . It tells of the miscegenation of divine and human beings which led to the rise of a mongrel race of superhuman attainments, frequently depicted as giants."

This type of analysis of the passage is frequently presented with a great degree of certainty. Vawter states that "there can be no doubt" that in the original version of the myth the sons of God were gods who cohabited with human women (p. 111).

In order to bridge the gap between pagan mythology and the religion of the Bible, one trend has been to analyze myth as "a way of presenting reality which has its proper place in the history of humankind" (Westermann, *Genesis 1–11*, 382). But as a "rose" is still a "rose" by any other name, so a myth is still a fictional creation of the human imagination that describes an event that occurs at every place and every time but also at no place and no time, despite repeated efforts to give the term a greater dignity. Because the redemptive history of the Bible describes real events that occurred to real people in real time, the category of myth can never serve as an appropriate vehicle for reporting the events of redemptive history. Westermann properly recognizes "the radical criticism of myth in the Old Testament" as well as "the fact that no myths originated in Israel" (p. 382). Yet he still asserts the presence of myth in the first half-verse of Gen. 6:4, even though he affirms that there is "nothing mythical" in the second half-verse (p. 378).

In the end, those who propose to treat this event as a myth can do so only because they do not intend to believe that Scripture records an event that actually occurred. Instead, the "event" reported must be "demythologized" to get at the "timeless truth" encapsulated in the myth. Once the reference to "gods" cohabiting with beautiful human women has been demythologized, then, according to one commentator, it may be understood that the real purpose of the fictional story is "to describe the overpowering force of human passion that brings people to overstep the limits set for them" (Westermann, *Genesis 1–11*, 381). But this demythologizing of a straightforward biblical narrative by introducing "gods" and then filtering them out again hardly may be regarded as an appropriate treatment of the record of redemptive history as it is reported in Scripture. Distinctive to the biblical faith in both its old covenant and its new covenant form are its opposition to polytheistic mythology, and its assertion that the one Creator-God remains distinct from his creation, even in an event as satiated with immanence as the incarnation.

12 This expression is paralleled by the phrase "sons of Elim," which appears to refer to angels in two passages in the psalms (Ps. 29:1; 89:7). This view also is a favorite, with individualized variations, of modern higher-critical interpreters. Gerhard von Rad in his commentary on Genesis (Philadelphia:

Westminister, 1976) introduces the section with the heading "The Angel Marriages" (p. 113). But to accommodate the Scriptures to his personal views, he must assert that the statement of Genesis 6:4 about the *nephilim* (interpreted as "giants") "*undoubtedly* once came [immediately] after v. 2 for these giants were, *of course,* the children of that marriage of heavenly beings with human women" (p. 115, italics added).

An unknown, unsung hero of the faith, Robert Gribble, who taught Old Testament at Austin Theological Seminary for many years, labeled these sweeping, unproved generalizations of unbelieving scholarship as "weasel words." If a theological point cannot be established by solid, careful exegesis, then an assertion must be covered by statements such as "all scholars agree that . . ." A classic example may be found in Julius Wellhausen's epoch-making popularization of the documentary hypothesis concerning the origins of the Pentateuch. He declares that with regard to the Jehovistic document, "all are happily agreed . . ."; and, "About the origin of Deuteronomy there is still less dispute; in all circles where appreciation of scientific results can be looked for at all, it is recognized that it was composed in the same age as that in which it was discovered" (Julius Wellhausen, *Prolegomena to the History of Ancient Israel* [New York: Meridian Books, 1957], 9).

In the case of von Rad's analysis of this passage, since the text of Scripture does not comply with his interpretation, he presumes to rearrange its statements so that it does. The reason he finds it necessary to make this rearrangement is that the biblical text as it presently stands does *not* affirm that the "heroes" of v. 4 were the offspring of a union "which is contrary to creation" (*Genesis,* 115).

13 Aalders, *Genesis,* 1:153, among others, rejects the view that the "sons of God" are angels.

14 The relationship established between the "sons of God" in Genesis 6 and the "daughters of men" is spelled out quite clearly when it is noted that they "took wives" of them. This phrase, "to take a wife," "is a standing expression throughout the Old Testament for the marriage relationship estab-

lished by God at creation, and is never applied to *porneia* [fornication], or the simple act of physical connection" (Keil and Delitzsch, *Biblical Commentary*, 1:131). The application of this kind of permanent relationship to angelic beings and humans goes well beyond the evidence of Scripture. Occasionally angels have manifested themselves for a brief time among men in the form of human bodies, as in the case of the three visitors to Abraham (Gen. 18:1–2). But if these beings were capable of sex, which is doubtful, it would have been their human side that would have possessed that capacity.

15 David Clines, "The Significance of the 'Sons of God' Episode in the Context of Primeval History," *Journal for the Study of the Old Testament* 13 (1979): 33ff., as cited in David Atkinson, *The Message of Genesis 1–11: The Dawn of Creation* (Leicester: Inter-Varsity, 1990), 130.

16 This viewpoint is supported by Aalders, *Genesis*, 1:154.

17 Elizabeth Goudge, *Green Dolphin Country* (London: Hodder and Stoughton, 1944). Perhaps more intriguing than the story itself is the fact that it is based on actual events. A man who had emigrated to another continent wrote home for his prospective bride after the lapse of a number of years. But he confused her name, and her sister sailed the seas to marry him. Still further, in real life the man also held his tongue and made his marriage work.

18 Aalders, *Genesis*, 2:119.

19 Keil and Delitzsch, *Biblical Commentary*, 1:289.

20 The text literally says, "Having eaten, he has eaten our silver." The expression "to eat money" still is used commonly in some parts of Africa. The phrase is quite descriptive. Apparently the meaning in the Genesis context is that Laban had squandered the dowry or the inheritance which should have benefited his daughters.

21 Laban's primary interest focuses on the whereabouts of his household gods. This concern may be explained by recent archaeological finds at a place called Nuzi. The ancient city of Nuzi was located east of the Tigris and Euphrates Rivers, about 200 miles north of Babylon. The site was excavated

in 1925–31. The city flourished in the second millennium B.C. Several thousand cuneiform tablets have been discovered, dating to the 15th–14th centuries B.C. According to these texts, "possession of the house gods could signify legal title to a given estate, particularly in cases out of the ordinary involving daughters, sons-in-law, or adopted sons" (Speiser, *Genesis*, 250). In accordance with Hurrian law, "Jacob's status in Laban's household would normally be tantamount to self-enslavement. That position, however, would be altered if Jacob was recognized as an adopted son who married the master's daughter. Possession of house gods might well have made the difference" (ibid.).

22 Vawter, *On Genesis*, 214; Speiser, *Genesis*, 120f.

23 Calvin, *Genesis*, 2:428.

24 Calvin, *Genesis*, 1:33, adopts the position that Abraham had been married to Keturah for some time before the death of Sarah. Keil and Delitzsch, *Biblical Commentary*, 1:261ff., are ambiguous on the matter. Keturah is called the "wife" of Abraham (Gen. 25:1), but she also is designated his "concubine" (1 Chron. 1:32; and by implication Gen. 25:5–6).

CHAPTER 3. SEX AND SUCCEEDING GENERATIONS

1 The Code of Hammurabi may provide some understanding of the situation. Hammurabi was the sixth king of the first dynasty of Babylon. He has been dated variously, but he most likely belongs in the eighteenth century B.C., which would coincide roughly with the time of the later patriarchs. Hammurabi's law-code is inscribed on a black stone that stands about eight feet high. Extensive writing is found on both sides of the pillar, which was set up in the temple of Marduk in Babylon. It represents the longest Babylonian inscription found to date. The document originally had about 4,000 lines, of which about 2,614 are still existent. At the top of the stele is a portrait of the king as he receives the law from the sun-god Shammash. About 240 of the original 282 laws still survive.

Paragraph 145 of the Code of Hammurabi states that a priestess who was free to marry but not to bear children could provide a slave-girl to her husband so he could have a son. But if the slave presumed to arrogate to herself a position of equality, the wife would have the power to demote her to her former slave rank (Bruce Vawter, *On Genesis: A New Reading* [Garden City, N.Y.: Doubleday, 1977], 120). The parallel with the Genesis narrative is quite apparent. Sarah provides a slave-girl for her husband because she can have no children. But the concubine apparently creates trouble for herself when she acts arrogantly.

Yet the differences from the Genesis narrative must also be noted. The provision of the Code of Hammurabi is limited in its application to certain priestesses. This restriction does not fit the circumstance of Abraham and Sarah. Though illuminating, the parallels with the Code of Hammurabi do not give the full picture as found in the Genesis narrative.

The Nuzi tablets also provide some instructive parallels with the Genesis narrative. In one case, a certain Shennima takes Gilimninu as his wife. If Gilimninu bears children, Shennima may not marry another woman. But if Gilimninu is barren, she shall provide her husband with a slave-girl. If any offspring arise from this merger, the original wife will have full control over the children (E. A. Speiser, *Genesis: Introduction, Translation, and Notes* [Garden City, N.Y.: Doubleday, 1964], 120–21). Similar procedures are still followed in many cultures today. If a wife does not bear children, she may bring her unmarried sister to her husband. If a child is born, it then becomes the possession of the original wife.

Sarah's harsh treatment of Hagar, the handmaid who has borne a son to Abraham, may also be illuminated by social customs of the day. According to the laws of the Nuzi tablets, a first wife cannot dismiss a slave-girl who has become her husband's wife. Correspondingly, in the biblical narrative Sarah does not dismiss Hagar. Instead, she makes her life so miserable by abusive treatment that Hagar flees.

2 Geerhardus. Vos, *Biblical Theology* (Edinburgh: Banner of Truth Trust, 1975), 81.

3 Gerhard von Rad, *Genesis: A Commentary* (Philadelphia: Westminster, 1976), 361, concludes that apparently Judah regarded Tamar as his daughter-in-law, and notes that the narrative comes to an end "without telling whose wife Tamar finally became." He raises the question as to whether she might have become the wife of Shelah, Judah's third son. But then he notes that the text simply does not say. Claus Westermann, *Genesis 1–11* (London: SPCK, 1984), 55, comments that a "relationship which would not have fulfilled the levirate obligation could be regarded as incest."

4 John Calvin, *Commentaries on the First Book of Moses Called Genesis* (Grand Rapids: Eerdmans, n.d.), 2:288f.

5 Some commentators attempt to limit this reference to great-grandsons. But the additional statement that distinguishes this experience from having his great-grandsons through Ephraim's brother Manasseh placed on his knees indicates that Joseph experienced the joy of seeing the sons of the sons of the sons of his son Ephraim. See C. F. Keil and F. Delitzsch, *Biblical Commentary on the Old Testament* (Grand Rapids: Eerdmans, n.d.), 1:412–13, who argue that there is no practical difficulty in this situation: "As Joseph's two sons were born before he was 37 years old (chap. 41:50), and Ephraim therefore was born, at the latest, in his 36th year, and possibly in his 34th, since Joseph was married in his 31st year, he might have had grandsons by the time he was 56 or 60 years old, and great-grandsons when he was from 78 to 85, so that great-great-grandsons might have been born when he was 100 or 110 years old." G. Ch. Aalders, *Genesis*, Bible Student's Commentary (Grand Rapids: Zondervan, 1981), 297–98, is more modest in his conclusions, suggesting only that Joseph must have seen his grandsons.

CHAPTER 4. SEX AND SIN

1 Derek Kidner, *Genesis: An Introduction and Commentary* (Leicester: Inter-Varsity, 1967), 78, remarks: "the savage disproportion of killing a mere lad (Hebrew *yeled* 'child') for a mere wound is the whole point of his boast."

But cf. Gordon J. Wenham, *Genesis 1–11* (Waco: Word, 1987), 1:114, who notes that in a passage like 1 Kings. 12:8, 10, a *yeled* possibly could denote someone as old as forty. However, the predominant usage of the term refers to a younger lad.

2 John Calvin, *Commentaries on the First Book Of Moses Called Genesis* (Grand Rapids: Eerdmans, n.d.), 1:217f.

3 O. Palmer Robertson, *Psalms in Congregational Celebration* (Durham: Evangelical Press, 1995), 182–87.

4 The last phrase of this prophetic pronouncement finds Jacob distancing himself from his son. Though not indicated in most translations, the phrasing changes abruptly from a second person "you went up" to a third person "he went up." See Kidner, *Genesis*, 216.

5 Gerhard von Rad, *Genesis: A Commentary* (Philadelphia: Westminister, 1976), 366, says the garment that Joseph left behind actually was his undergarment, "a long shirt tied about the hips," for men did not normally wear their cloaks indoors. Concludes von Rad: "This means that Joseph fled completely undressed, at once disgracefully and honorably." But the term used in the narrative is the common Hebrew word for "garment" (*beged*). The Septuagint translates *himatia*, which is commonly used to refer to an outer cloak in distinction from an inner garment.

6 Randy Thornhill and Craig T. Palmer, *A Natural History of Rape*, as quoted in *Guardian Weekly*, 6–12 April 2000, p. 23.

7 G. Ch. Aalders, *Genesis*, Bible Student's Commentary (Grand Rapids: Zondervan, 1981), 2:154.

8 C. F. Keil and F. Delitzsch, *Biblical Commentary on the Old Testament* (Grand Rapids: Eerdmans, n.d.), 1:311, estimate her age at between thirteen and fifteen years.

9 Gordon J. Wenham, *Genesis 16–50* (Waco: Word, 1994), 2:312.

10 Benno Jacob, *The First Book of the Bible: Genesis* (New York: Ktav, 1974), 232.

11 Von Rad, *Genesis*, 332.

12 Calvin, *Genesis*, 2:220.

13 Keil and Delitzsch, *Biblical Commentary*, 1:237.

14 E. A. Speiser, *Genesis: Introduction, Translation, and Notes* (Garden City, N.Y.: Doubleday, 1964), 145, proposes that this perspective should lead to praise for Lot's daughters rather than blame for their action. This analysis is not quite convincing.

15 Von Rad, *Genesis*, 224.

16 Jacob, *First Book*, 129.

17 D. Sherwin Bailey in *Homosexuality and the Western Christian Tradition* (Hamden, Conn.: Archon, 1975), 2–5, argues that the verb "to know" in this passage does not refer to a sexual relationship. For a thorough refutation of this interpretation, see Kidner, *Genesis*, 136.

18 Jacob, *First Book*, 125, supposes that Lot's offer of his daughters should not be taken seriously, since he knew well their depraved appetites. But it would seem more likely that Lot had been affected seriously in his moral judgments by his constant interchange with a community as depraved as Sodom.

19 Von Rad, *Genesis*, 218.

20 The idea that the African people are a cursed community as a consequence of their being descendants of Ham has no biblical basis. Scripture clearly states that Canaan rather than Ham was cursed. The idea that the son was cursed rather than the father who committed the crime presents certain difficulties. But such a problem is not resolved by ignoring the clear statement of Scripture that Canaan rather than Ham was cursed. For further discussion of the subject, see O. Palmer Robertson, "Current Critical Questions Concerning the 'Curse of Ham' (Genesis 9:20–27)," *Journal of the Evangelical Theological Society* (June 1998), 177–88.

21 Aalders, *Genesis*, 2:15, says that the wickedness of Sodom "had reached the worst extremes."

22 David Atkinson, *The Message of Genesis 1–11* (Leicester: Inter-Varsity, 1990), 78.

CHAPTER 5. SEX AND SINGLENESS

1 Contra Claus Westermann, *Genesis 1–11: A Commentary* (London: SPCK, 1984), 232.

2 Walter Wangerin Jr., *As for Me and My House: Crafting Your Marriage to Last* (Nashville: Thomas Nelson, 1990), 23f.

3 The term *levirate* refers to the customary law that stated that if a man died childless, a brother of his was obligated to marry the widow in order to raise up children in the name of his deceased brother.

4 This second son of Judah, whose name was Onan, has given the name "onanism" to the act of male masturbation. But as has been noted, the action of Onan in this narrative was not onanism, but *coitus interruptus*. Yet the narrative would imply that the actual sin of Onan was his selfish refusal to raise up a seed to his deceased brother. Cf. Bruce Vawter, *On Genesis* (Garden City, N.Y.: Doubleday, 1977), 395.

5 See Derek Kidner, *Genesis: An Introduction and Commentary* (Leicester: Inter-Varsity, 1967), 188f. Says Kidner: "Such was the world into which Judah had married."

6 See Benno Jacob, *The First Book of the Bible: Genesis* (New York: Ktav, 1974), 262.

CHAPTER 6. SEX AND THE
END OF THIS LIFE

1 G. Ch. Aalders, *Genesis*, Bible Student's Commentary (Grand Rapids: Zondervan, 1981), 2:59, notes that in comparison with land prices as determined by archaeological finds, the four hundred shekels charged to Abraham was excessively high. Ephron the Hittite was taking full advantage of Abraham's desperate situation.

INDEX OF
SCRIPTURE

O. Palmer Robertson (B.D., Westminster Theological Seminary; Th.M., Th.D., Union Theological Seminary, Virginia) is professor of Old Testament at Knox Theological Seminary and professor of theology at African Bible College, Malawi.

He previously taught at Reformed, Covenant, and Westminster Theological Seminaries, has served as pastor of four congregations, and has also lectured in Asia, Europe, and Latin America.

Among his many published works are *The Christ of the Covenants*, *The Israel of God: Yesterday, Today, and Tomorrow*, and *Understanding the Land of the Bible*.